FASHIONING FEMININITIES, MAKING MASCULINITIES

Christina Sunardi

FASHIONING FEMININITIES, MAKING MASCULINITIES

Gender, Performance, and Lived Experience in Java, Indonesia

The Gender Studies Collection

Collection Editors

Jan Etienne & Reham El Morally

LPp

First published in 2024 by Lived Places Publishing

The author and editors have made every effort to ensure the accuracy of information contained in this publication, but assume no responsibility for any errors, inaccuracies, inconsistencies and omissions. Likewise, every effort has been made to contact copyright holders. If any copyright material has been reproduced unwittingly and without permission the Publisher will gladly receive information enabling them to rectify any error or omission in subsequent editions.

British Library Cataloguing in Publication Data
A CIP record for this book is available from the British Library

ISBN: 9781916704190 (pbk)
ISBN: 9781916704213 (ePDF)
ISBN: 9781916704206 (ePUB)

The right of Christina Sunardi to be identified as the Author of this work has been asserted by them in accordance with the Copyright, Design and Patents Act 1988.

Cover design by Fiachra McCarthy
Book design by Rachel Trolove of Twin Trail Design
Typeset by Newgen Publishing UK

Lived Places Publishing
Long Island
New York 11789

www.livedplacespublishing.com

Gunung Semèru daerah Malang,
Munggah mudhun iku dalané.
Nèk digugu aja gumampang,
Cèk dipercaya karo kancané.

(Mount Semèru in the Malang area,
Up and down goes the road.
If trusted, do not take it lightly,
So that you are believed by your friends.)

(East Javanese poetic text as learned from
the dancer Sumi'anah,
May 5, 2006.
Translated from the Javanese with help from
the musician Stefanus Yacobus Suryantono,
May 2006.)

Abstract

This book explores the production and negotiation of gender and local identity in the regency of Malang in the cultural region of east Java, Indonesia through traditional performing arts and lived experiences of dancers who have participated in the performance of cross-gender dance. Drawing on ethnographic fieldwork conducted in and visits to Malang spanning 2004 to 2015, I present ways performers have navigated cultural norms to make sense of and articulate gender and senses of place-based identity on- and offstage in a Muslim-majority context.

Keywords

contingency of gender, cross-gender dance, gamelan, gender fluidity, gender pluralism, female masculinity, Islam, male femininity, spirituality, *waria*

Note on terms of address

I have chosen mostly not to use honorifics—which are very important in speaking Indonesian and Javanese politely—because their usage is not fixed. The appropriate term of address one person uses when speaking to another is determined by their relationship, their social status at a particular moment, the context, and other factors. For example, a person I may address as "father" or "mother", another person may address as "brother" or "sister". I mean no disrespect by not using honorifics (Sunardi, 2015, p. x).

Acknowledgments

As in all my endeavors, I have been generously supported by numerous people and institutions in the writing of this book. The research was funded at various stages by a Fulbright-Hays Doctoral Dissertation Research Abroad Fellowship; a University of California Office of the President Pacific Rim Mini Grant; University of California, Berkeley Center for Southeast Asia Studies Grant-In-Aid Scholarships; and a University of California, Berkeley Graduate Division Travel Award. The writing was generously supported by two University of Washington professorships, an Adelaide D. Currie Cole Endowed Professorship in the School of Music, and a Floyd & Delores Jones Endowed Professorship in the Arts. I remain grateful to Didik Nini Thowok and LPK Tari Natya Lakshita, M. Soleh Adi Pramono and the Mangun Dharma Art Center (Padepokan Seni Mangun Dharma [PSMD]), and the Indonesian Institute of Sciences (Lembaga Ilmu Pengetahuan Indonesia [LIPI]) for sponsoring me in Indonesia. Many thanks to David Wolbrecht for drawing the beautiful maps. I am thankful to Jan Etienne for providing feedback and guidance through this project as well as to David Parker and the larger publishing team—including the collection editors—at Lived Places Publishing for their vision, comments, and encouragement. I thank my husband Sunardi for his ongoing loving patience and support and my daughter Esther for the sunshine she brings to my life. Any shortcomings, misinterpretations, or errors that remain are my own.

Contents

1
Introduction and learning objectives

Singing and dancing female figures dominate the make-shift stage characteristic of outdoor performances of lud-ruk theater. The sounds of the accompanying gamelan music played on an ensemble largely comprised of metal keyed instruments and gongs pierce the air through an enormous sound system: interlocking octaves pop; lines of melody sparkle; powerful drum strokes articulate the dancers' delicate yet powerfully precise movements. The incessant "chrings" of their ankle bells add a layer of color, life, intensity, and magic. Some watching whistle with delight and desire; others whisper their wonder. While some of the dancers are perhaps in their thirties, ripe in their sexuality, others are older, exuding a more mature womanliness no less stunning. While some are slender and others are not—some shy, some coy, some confident, some detached—each interprets the drumming in their own way as they dance not quite together with the others; their femininity engulfs, mesmerizes, and arouses despite the maleness of their bodies.

A tayub event is no less remarkable. Rows of guests, mostly men, sit at long tables awaiting their turns to request a song and dance with the female singer-dancers who have been hired to entertain them. The women have enhanced their beauty by carefully applying thick false eyelashes; drawing exquisite mustaches above their full, red lips; and donning wigs of neat, short hair. Seemingly unimpressed by the guests when they perform, the dancers move to the sounds of the gamelan with a strong sort of grace, their lolloping head rolls and martial-arts-like moves enhanced by bass drum and cymbal crashes, the gamelan supplemented with a keyboard to appeal to the tastes of audiences who enjoy popular forms of music. Despite the masculinity that the movement and music evoke, the powerful womanliness of the dancers' figures and voices overwhelms. An earthiness permeates the damp, humid air already heavy with snaking tendrils of cigarette smoke, already pregnant with the smells of cloves, tobacco, mud, alcohol, and sweat.

* * *

Come! I invite you to delve into males' embodiment of femininity and females' embodiment of masculinity in the cultural region of east Java, Indonesia, where I conducted field research on dance and its accompanying gamelan music and where I visited over the course of 2004 to 2015, with a period of intensive fieldwork spanning 2005 to 2007. Captivated by the fashioning of femininities and the making of masculinities, I have been inspired to write about the negotiation of gender through dance performance (Sunardi, 2009; 2011; 2013; 2015; 2020; 2022). My admiration of the artists I consulted and saw perform continues to fuel me as I build on my prior work to offer this intentionally short book meant for use in undergraduate courses. As such, this book addresses the questions:

1.   How is gender a cultural construction that people continuously produce, reproduce, contest, challenge, alter, and so on—in short, negotiate?
2.   How can we understand processes by and through which individuals negotiate gender through the performing arts and their lived experiences as artists in specific cultural contexts?

I offer answers to these questions—recognizing that these are not the only answers—by establishing my analytical and methodological approaches in this chapter and, in the following two chapters, by centering the lived experiences and perspectives of six dancers in the east Javanese regency of Malang. I argue that through both their onstage participation in cross-gender dance performance and through their offstage lives they contributed to the cultural production of gender, and in doing so, they contributed to the production of local place-based identity. Chapter 2 focuses on ways in which two men and one *waria* (a male who dresses and lives as female) produced complex senses of gender through the performance of female-style dance since the mid-twentieth century. Chapter 3 presents three women who produced complex senses of gender through the performance of male-style dance through the course of the twentieth century (perhaps since the late 1890s) and into the twenty-first. In addition to onstage–offstage implications, themes that link Chapters 2 and 3 include gender fluidity, gender pluralism, and spirituality. Chapters 2 and 3 are framed by learning objectives and questions for discussion. These questions are very much meant as a place to start and I encourage you to develop additional questions for discussion, reflection, and additional research. I conclude the book with some closing words, and then suggest discussion questions pertinent to the entire book as well as project or assignment ideas. A short list of recommended further readings follows the list of references at the end of the book, although I do recommend every source in the reference list as well! But before we get to all of that, let's get our bearings.

Malang as a place

Malang is a regency (*kabupaten*; analogous to a county in the Unites States) and city in the cultural region of east Java, one of several cultural regions within the Indonesian province of East Java (Figure 1). Unless I specify otherwise, I am referring to Malang as a whole—the city and regency together—when I write Malang. I use the approach of the ethnomusicologist R. Anderson Sutton (1985; 1991) to distinguish national political divisions from cultural regions as the two do not always match: lower-case letters refer to cultural regions (such as east Java and central Java) while upper-case letters refer to names of Indonesian provinces (such as East Java and Central Java). The traditions of music, dance, and theater that musicians and dancers referred to as east Javanese are rooted in the central part of the province of East Java, including the cities of Malang, Mojokerto, Jombang, and Surabaya and their surrounding areas (Sutton, 1991, p. 121; Sunardi, 2010, pp. 89, 120n3; 2015, p. ix; 2017, p. 65; 2020, p. 448; 2023, p. 8; in press). Banyuwangi at the eastern tip of Java and the island of Madura to the north

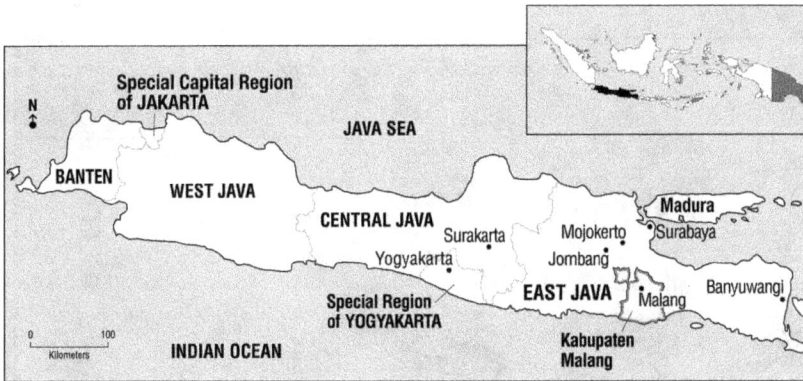

Figure 1. Map showing Malang as well as provinces, special regions, and selected cities of Java. Map drawn by David Wolbrecht, © 2013 University of Washington.

each have their own traditions of performing arts (Sutton, 1991, pp. 121–122; Crawford, 2001, p. 329). As one moves west from Malang, the performing arts traditions become increasingly similar to those of central Java. When performers in Malang spoke about central Javanese arts, they were usually referring to the arts associated with Surakarta within the province of Central Java, sometimes including Yogyakarta in the Special Region of Yogyakarta (Sutton, 1991, pp. 19–68, 121; Sunardi, 2010, p. 89; 2015, p. x; 2017, p. 65; 2023, p. 11). I resided about 23 kilometers east of the city of Malang in the village of Tulusbesar (or Tulus Besar), studying gamelan music and dance primarily with artists in the subdistricts of Tumpang and Poncokusuma, and also interviewing performers and observing performances in the city of Malang (Figure 2).

Malang was a stimulating place, visually and culturally. I regularly saw breathtaking hills and mountains, including an active

Figure 2. Map showing the village of Tulusbesar, the subdistricts of Tumpang and Poncokusuma, and the city of Malang within the regency of Malang. Map drawn by David Wolbrecht, © 2013 University of Washington.

volcano visible in the distance, agricultural fields, apple orchards, rivers, streams, ruins of thirteenth- and fourteenth-century temples, ducks, chickens, goats, cats, dogs, small horses, and more, all of which constantly reminded me of the importance of the land and animals in sustaining life and culture in the area over the centuries. The diverse ethnic makeup, including Javanese, Chinese, Madurese, and various multi-ethnic people and families contributed to a rich multi-cultural fabric. Religious diversity was no less noticeable. While predominately Muslim, Christianity was also present—one of my teachers was Catholic. Hinduism was also practiced, particularly in the Tengger mountain communities that span the regencies of Malang, Pasuruan, Probolinggo, and Lumajang (Hefner, 1985, p. 44). Javanese spiritual beliefs and practices were very present, sometimes comprising part of what the anthropologist Timothy Daniels refers to as the Islamic spectrum in Java to capture the variety of approaches to Islam, ways of being Muslim, and ways of expressing Islamic piety in Java (2009). Indeed, spirituality is a theme that permeates this book.

I found the people I met and worked with in the village environments of Tumpang and Poncokusuma to be quite cosmopolitan. Most were fairly current on national and international events through television, newspapers, word of mouth, and, for younger generations, social media. Those interested in fashion and celebrity gossip were also up to date on those matters. Cell phones and texting were a regular part of life, particularly for the younger people. People in Tumpang and Poncokusuma frequently traveled to the city of Malang for various reasons, such as to work, shop, attend school, and for fun. Many had also traveled to other parts of Java, other parts of Indonesia, and/or to other countries for various reasons, including to work and to visit family. Some had family members who had traveled. I met or heard about a few people who had made the haj, the Muslim pilgrimage to Mecca (Sunardi, 2015, pp. xv–xvii). It was in the dynamic context of Malang as a place with its stunning beauty and engaging individuals that I had the privilege of studying local styles of performance.

Importance of place

Malang as a place was critically important to most of the 60 or so performers I consulted, including dancers, musicians, and puppeteers/masked dance narrators. Most consistently emphasized their performance practices, traditions, and identities as Malangan—a distinct substyle and identity within east Java. Within Malang, they distinguished styles and ways of performing music and dance associated with different areas, and differences within areas at the levels of villages and in some cases individuals (Sunardi, 2010, pp. 89, 90–91; 2015, pp. xxii–xxiii).

Many voiced concerns that their local styles of performance (music, dance, theater) would disappear as they were replaced by the more popular and prestigious traditional styles from central Java and Surabaya and by genres of popular music. Such genres of popular music included *dangdut*, which features electric guitar(s), bass, keyboard(s), and drums at its core, often with flute (Frederick, 1982; Manuel, 1988, pp. 210–211; Yampolsky, 1991; Weintraub, 2010), and *campur sari*, which combines gamelan instruments with electric keyboards, bass, and guitar, among other instruments depending on the group (Brinner, 2008, p. 19; Supanggah, 2003; Cooper, 2015). The artists I consulted in Malang felt that their arts had been marginalized, underrep-resented, and, due to audience preferences and demands for central Javanese, Surabayan, and popular forms, local Malangan styles would eventually vanish (Sunardi, 2010, pp. 93–94; 2015, pp. 22–25).

The artists I worked with were thus heavily invested in preserving their local styles of performance, which they sought to do in part by working with me—having me document their traditions and their experiences and taking this material to share with others in the United States through my writing and teaching as a pro-fessor, which indeed I have done my best to do. One significant takeaway from my fieldwork—from listening to performers—is that the production and representation of gender through dance performance was integrally connected to performers' senses of their local, place-based identities. In other words, I found that the production of gender and place-based identity were intri-cately connected, one informing the other, as performers strove to maintain Malangan styles of music, dance, and theater as dis-tinct substyles within the cultural region of east Java. This point, a key component of the main argument of this book, builds from the argument in my first book that through changes perform-ers made to tradition, they negotiated culturally constructed boundaries of gender and sex (2015, p. 1) as well as my attention to the production of senses of place and local identity through the performing arts (2010; 2015; 2017; 2020; 2023).

My thinking about the roles of the performing arts in the pro-duction and representation of place-based identities has been enriched by the work of Martin Stokes, R. Anderson Sutton, and Zoila Mendoza, among other scholars. Martin Stokes, an ethnomusicologist, argues that "music and dance … provide the means by which the hierarchies of place are negotiated and transformed" (1994, p. 4). He goes on to write that music (and dance, I add) are "socially meaningful not entirely but largely because [they provide] means by which people recognize identities and places, and the boundaries which separate them" (1994, p. 5). The anthropologist Zoila Mendoza investigates dance troupes' performances during patron saint festivals in Peru as a form of ritual dance that produces complex senses of identity in relation to notions of place, history, ethnicity/race (one complex category), gender, generation, and class (2000). Similarly, R. Anderson Sutton, also an ethnomusicologist, focuses on multiple senses of identity produced through performance as he investigates South Sulawesians' presentations of themselves as belonging to a region, as a particular ethnicity, as modern, and as part of the Indonesian nation through dance and music (2002). In earlier work on gamelan traditions in different regions of Java—including in east Java and Malang—he examines expressions of place-specific identity through analysis of performance practice and institutions, work that I have extended in my analyses of Malangan and east Javanese gamelan performance practices (Sutton, 1985; 1991; Sunardi, 2010, pp. 91–92; 2011; 2015; 2017; 2020; 2023).

Performing arts in Malang

The performing arts that I studied in Malang fall into what performers categorized as "traditional" (*tradisi*), including gamelan music and dance accompanied by gamelan music. Gamelan are ensembles comprised largely of gongs, keyed percussion instruments, and drum(s) (Figure 3). Vocal parts may also be used and sometimes featured, and other instruments such as zither, bowed fiddle, and bamboo flute may also be used. Gamelan ensembles of various types can be found on the Indonesian islands of Java, Madura, Bali, and Lombok. Similar types of ensembles are played in other areas of Southeast Asia as well, such as *piphat* in Thailand, *pinpeat* in Cambodia, *saing waing* in Myanmar/Burma, and *kulintang* in the Philippines (Kalanduyan, 1996; Spiller, 2008, pp. 23–38; Douglas, 2010). In Java, the metal that is usually preferred for the gongs and metal keyed instruments in a gamelan is bronze, although iron and brass, which are less expensive, may also be used (Brinner, 2008, p. 3). As

Figure 3. This photograph shows several instruments of a gamelan ensemble. Photograph taken by the author, 2006.

indicated, there are different regional styles, and different styles within regions.

Among other purposes, gamelan music in Java is used to accompany dance, including forms of masked and non-masked dance, dance events called *tayub* or *tayuban* in which professional female entertainers are hired to sing and dance for a host's guests, hobby-horse dance events that often feature dancers going into a trance (*jaranan*), and various forms of theater, including shadow puppet theater (*wayang kulit*), masked dance drama (*wayang topèng*), and *ludruk*, a form of east Javanese theater that features a variety of opening acts and a main play or drama. Performing art forms such as these are typically sponsored by a host (which could be an individual, a family, a community, a business, and so on) to celebrate a certain occasion, such as a wedding, the circumcision of a boy marking his transition to manhood, the opening of a business, an anniversary (such as the founding of a community or organization), a holiday, an auspicious day on the Javanese calendar, and village-cleansing ceremonies. Music, dance, and theater may also be featured at festivals and competitions, and in other contexts.

This book focuses on the dances *Beskalan*, *Ngremo* (*Ngrema*, *Ngrémo*, *Remo*), and masked dance, which exist in both male (*lanang*, *putra*, *pria*) and female (*putri*, *wanita*) styles. Male-style dances are characterized in general by wider stances, higher arm positions, and larger movement volumes than female-style dances (Figures 4 and 5). Male-style dances include *Beskalan Lanang*, *Ngremo Lanang* (also referred to as *Ngremo Putra*, *Ngremo Pria*), and masked dances that portray males. Female-style dances include *Beskalan Putri*, *Ngremo Putri* (also referred to

Figure 4. The dancer Tri Wahyuningtyas poses in a position from the male-style dance *Beskalan Lanang* in costume. Photograph taken by the author, 2009.

Figure 5. The dancer Wahyu Winarti poses in a position from the female-style dance *Beskalan Putri* in costume. Photograph taken by the author, 2006.

as *Ngremo Wanita*), and masked dances that portray female characters. *Beskalan*, *Ngremo*, and masked dances may be performed as opening or welcoming dances for other performances or events—such as an opening dance for a puppet performance, *ludruk*, or *tayub* (although typically when an opening dance is used for *tayub* it is *Ngremo*). Masked dances may also be performed in the context of masked dance drama. *Ngremo* dancers often sing in the course of performing the dance, welcoming audiences and/or guests and singing a form of poetry called *parikan*, such as the epigraph of this book, among other texts (Sunardi, 2015, pp. 17, 51-54, 81-82; 2023). While historically *Beskalan* dancers also sang in the course of performing the dance, this had largely fallen out of typical practice at the time of my fieldwork and visits to Malang (Sunardi, 2015, pp. 127-157).

Cross-gender performance

Male-style dances in Java are not exclusively performed by male dancers and female-style dances are not exclusively performed by female dancers. The dancer Tri Wahyuningtyas, posing in a position from the male-style dance *Beskalan Lanang* in Figure 4, for example, is a woman that you will meet again in Chapter 3. A person's body type as well as their personality and disposition tended to be considered in relation to what dances they were steered towards performing by teachers, mentors, and consumers—that is, what patrons requested or hired them for, among other factors. Individuals were also drawn to certain dances based on affinities they felt for the dance. For example, a dance may resonate with a dancer's own personality, disposition, and ways of moving. Indeed, performing dances as cross-gender dance in Malang—both women performing male-style dance and men or *waria* performing female-style dance—was common and for some dances was expected.

Cross-gender performance has had multiple meanings in east Java and related cultural regions. On one end of the spectrum, it has been an accepted practice integral to local worldviews. Traditions of cross-gender performance in masked dance, social dance, and popular theater have existed throughout what is now the province of East Java since at least the 1820s and early twentieth century (Pigeaud, 1938, pp. 277, 301, 321–323, 328). Paul Wolbers (1989; 1993) and R. Anderson Sutton (1993) link boys' performance of female-style dance for ritual ceremonies in Banyuwangi to centuries-old Hindu and indigenous Javanese imagery in which androgyny represents cosmic power and fertility. There are also historical and contemporary examples of cross-gender performance, both males performing female-style dance and vice versa, in Central Java and West Java (Sunardi, 2015, pp. 20–21). For example, males performed female-style dance in central Javanese contexts, including eighteenth-, nineteenth-, and twentieth-century courts (Raffles, 1988, p. 342; Ponder, 1990, p. 134; Hughes-Freeland, 1995, p. 184; 2006, pp. 65–66; 2008b, pp. 154–157; Sumarsam, 1995, p. 276n59).

On the other end of the spectrum, cross-gender performance has been a strategy that individuals have employed to negotiate official Indonesian constructions of manhood and womanhood. Influenced by Javanese aristocratic, Dutch colonial, and Islamic norms, dominant Indonesian constructions have tended to separate maleness from femaleness, link gender to biological sex in a one-to-one mapping—masculinity to male bodies to man, femininity to female bodies to woman—and privilege heterosexuality, shaping gender ideologies the Indonesian government has promoted since the declaration of independence in 1945 (Blackwood 2005: 866, 869–871; 2007: 185–188; Sunardi 2009; 2013; 2015; 2020; 2022). In a nutshell, dominant, state-promoted constructions of ideal masculinity promoted larger-bodied, physically stronger-looking masculine figures as men were encouraged to assume positions of leadership within the nation as political leaders and lawmakers and within the family as household heads (Shiraishi, 1997, pp. 90–91; Wieringa, 2002, p. 99; Spiller, 2010, p. 26). Women were encouraged to be refined, polite, quiet, and dedicated to the home and their social roles as wives supporting their husbands and as mothers raising their children (Shiraishi, 1997, pp. 90–91; Wieringa, 2002, pp. 99, 130–132; Sunardi, 2009, pp. 462–463; 2015, p. 38).

By embodying the gendered characteristics associated with the opposite sex onstage and/or in their daily lives, males and females in many parts of Indonesia have resisted dominant constructions, as discussed in the work of scholars such as Evelyn Blackwood (2005), Benedict Anderson (1996), Dédé Oetomo (1996), Tom Boellstorff (2004a; 2004b), Jan Mrázek (2005), Herry Gendut Janarto (2005), Setiyono Wahyudi and G.R. Lono Lastoro Simatupang (2005), and Felicia Hughes-Freeland (2008a; 2008b, pp. 161–162). Individuals in Indonesia have contended with multiple logics and meanings of cross-gender performance in different ways in diverse contexts, articulating senses of masculinity and femininity for a variety of reasons. In so doing, as I show in this book about dancers and dance in Malang, performers have contributed to complicated expectations about cross-gender representation. While performers have resisted dominant norms in terms of what type of bodies produce and embody what gender, performers have also reinforced dominant norms, such as norms of behaviors, ways of moving, and ways of sounding that constitute ideal senses of femininity and masculinity.

Similarly, cross-gender performance in various Asian traditions has provided cultural space in and through which performers have navigated, negotiated, challenged, and reaffirmed dominant gender norms and ideologies. A few of these traditions, each with rich and complex histories, include Chinese opera, in which males have performed female roles and vice versa (Rao, 2002, pp. 408, 413, 416; Li, 2003; Lau, 2008, pp. 67, 70, 73), Japanese *kabuki* theater in which male actors have specialized in female roles (Wade, 2005, pp. 114–115; Isaka, 2016), and the Japanese Takarazuka Revue company in which females have played male roles (Robertson, 1998; Solander, 2023). Indeed, performance is an important site in which to explore the production and negotiation of gender.

Gender and the performing arts

A focus on performers and performance offers a critical means to explore and examine ways in which individuals produce and represent complex senses of gender. Onstage, people may take on a persona, express themselves through a performed persona, and/or push at dominant norms in ways that they would not do in offstage daily life. In some cases, transgressing dominant norms is culturally and socially accepted onstage but not in daily life. Transgressing dominant norms onstage has the potential to change ideas about what is socially acceptable in daily life as people become more used to seeing it onstage. Performance can thereby open cultural space for change. Performance also provides a window into the production of gender because performers' manipulations of their bodies are particularly exposed and conventions of embodying, producing, and representing femininities and masculinities are particularly visible. Performance denaturalizes gender because it makes the reality that gender is a construction and an enactment—rather than inherent—more transparent, a point I draw from Judith Butler's analysis of drag (1999, p. 175; Sunardi, 2015, pp. 14–15).

I foreground the agency of artists who perform cross-gender dance as individuals who produce complex constructions of gender through performance and play critical social roles that affect local senses of identity. On the one hand, they may reify mainstream cultural norms in Malang by performing ideal constructions of "male" and "female" in terms of physical appearance, behavior, and social position through established dance forms. On the other hand, they may simultaneously undermine a one-to-one mapping of biological sex and gender role. They may further challenge norms through the different personas they embody when performing onstage and when living their daily lives. This is not to say, however, that dancers do not have many reasons for performing cross-gender dance—including earning a living.

Analytical approaches to gender

My approaches to thinking about gender have been influenced by many scholars, only a few of whom I discuss here. From the gender theorist Judith Butler (1990; 1993; 1999), mentioned above, I have built on the notion of gender performativity—that gender is an unstable cultural construction that is produced by and through what a person does. In other words, a person is not a gender because of the biological sex they were assigned at birth, but because of what a person does to be and identify as a gender, which can change and shift. "Doing" a gender—or performing a gender broadly speaking and not just on a stage in a theatrical sense but also in daily life—may include how a person dresses, acts, speaks, does their hair, wears makeup (or not), and so on. It is important to recognize that a person does and thereby produces their gender in relation to many other facets of their identity, as the theoretical framework of intersectionality emphasizes; such facets that intersect with gender include but are not limited to a person's ethnicity and/or race, class, age, generation, national identity, regional identity, religion, political affiliation, and so on—categories that, like gender, are also fluid and products of complex webs of power (Crenshaw, 1991; Nash, 2008; Cho, Crenshaw, and McCall, 2013, p. 795; see also Del Negro and Berger, 2004). Cultural and historical context, including the place(s) where people live, work, and spend free time are thus critical in understanding how individuals negotiate gender in particular ways.

Butler's argument that it is the repetition of cultural norms that makes many people believe that the norms are natural and normal, rather than cultural constructions that people create, has also shaped my thinking (1999, p. 12). The potential for some aspect of the repetition to differ from previous repetitions, however, does allow space for change (1993, p. 234). In other words, adjustments people as active agents make to the way they do a gender in a particular context can lead to changes in what are culturally acceptable (or contested) ways of being—or doing—that gender. Such adjustments and changes may range from subtle to radical. Perhaps you can think of some examples.

An equally influential point that I have taken from Butler's work is that biological sex, in addition to gender, is culturally constructed (1990, p. 275; 1993, pp. 1–2; 1999, pp. 10–11). That is, the ways people understand biological sex, what comprises biological sex, how many sexes exist, and so on, are culturally constructed. Butler's work has helped me to formulate ideas about how gender and biological sex are performed, articulated, created, and negotiated by artists in Malang both onstage as performers and offstage as they live their lives. Artists thereby impact and create or produce culture at large. Another way to put this is that artists contribute to cultural production, including the cultural production of gender. Butler and others also importantly acknowledge that while cross-gender performance can challenge what types of bodies can embody, represent, and produce which genders, cross-gender performance can also reinforce dominant norms, as I have mentioned earlier. For example, a person assigned male at birth performing hyper-femininity on stage as a drag artist may reinforce dominant social pressures for how women should look, sound, and act (Peacock, 1987, pp. 168–172; Butler, 1993, pp. 125, 231, 237; Anderson, 1996; Shaw, 2005, p. 16).

The gender studies scholar Judith Halberstam (now Jack Halberstam) and the anthropologist Tom Boellstorff have provided approaches and vocabulary to identify and analyze complex senses of gender in Malang. Halberstam has offered the concept of female masculinity—senses of masculinity that are

produced, owned, and embodied by female bodies and differ from male masculinities (1998, pp. 1–2, 15; Blackwood and
Wieringa, 2007, pp. 9, 14–15; Blackwood, 2010, p. 29; Sunardi,
2013, p. 141; 2015, p. 11; 2022, p. 290). From Tom Boellstorff I have
taken an analogous concept of male femininity—senses of femininity produced, owned, and embodied by male bodies (2004b;
2005b, pp. 169, 171, 175; 2007, pp. 82, 99, 108; Sunardi, 2013,
p. 141; 2015, p. 11; 2022, p. 290).

A male–female gender binary or spectrum in many ways is still
assumed or maintained through terms such as female masculinity and male femininity (Sunardi, 2015, pp. 10–11). In the cultural context of Malang (and Indonesia more broadly speaking),
that binary is strong and, in addition to female masculinity and
male femininity, the concepts of "male" and "female", "man" and
"woman", "masculinity" and "femininity" have been useful, as
Boellstorff highlights for Southeast Asia in general (2007, p. 208).
At the same time there is also gender fluidity as people move
between different ways of doing gender, and gender pluralism,
which the anthropologist Michael Peletz explains:

> includes pluralistic sensibilities and dispositions regard-
> ing bodily practices (adornment, attire, mannerisms) and
> embodied desires, as well as social roles, sexual relation-
> ships, and ways of being that bear on or are otherwise
> linked with local conceptions of femininity, masculinity,
> androgyny, etc. (2006, p. 310)

Gender fluidity and gender pluralism are two additional interre-
lated themes that thread this book.

Complicating the gender binary in Indonesia is the *waria* gender identity or category. I recognize that using English terms for *waria* presents challenges, as discussed by Tom Boellstorff. For example, since the *waria* he consulted "usually see themselves as originating from the category 'man' and as remaining men in some fashion", he found that the terms transgender and transsexual fell short in capturing how they understood themselves (2007, p. 82). Additional challenges of using English terms include the continuous emergence of new vocabulary in transgender studies, the array of terms transgender people use to identify themselves in English-speaking contexts such as the United States, and differing attitudes among transgender people about the same terms; what one person may find respectable another may find insulting (Green, Denny, and Cromwell, 2018, pp. 100, 106). Terminology also changes in Indonesia. More recently, in 2014 and 2015, Benjamin Hegarty found that *waria* understand the English word transgender and that some use it in Yogyakarta and Jakarta, places frequented by foreign researchers and journalists who may have contributed to its usage (2017, pp. 78–79).

The gloss that I use for *waria*—males who dress and live as female—is meant to communicate the male femininity that is a key part of *waria* identity for many and to allow for the recognition of *waria* as a gender category that is distinct from that of "woman" (Oetomo, 2000, p. 50; Boellstorff 2004b; 2005b; 2007; Sunardi, 2015, pp. 63–93). At the same time, I do not mean to imply that there is any one way of living as female or identifying as a woman, that all males who live as female necessarily identify as *waria* rather than as women, or that identifying as a *waria* and as a woman is mutually exclusive. Hegarty analyzes an interview with a group of *waria* in which one, for example, does refer to herself as a woman (2017, p. 86; Sunardi, 2022, pp. 296–297).

Evelyn Blackwood's and others' writing about the enactment of gender being dependent on context has also influenced my analytical approach—that is, that people may do gender in different ways in different situations—and I extend Blackwood's concept of "contingent masculinity" to think through instances of contingent male femininity, contingent female masculinity, and the contingency of gender more broadly speaking (2010, p. 21; Oetomo, 2000, p. 50; Boellstorff, 2007, p. 100, Sunardi, 2013, p. 141; 2015, p. 11). For example, a person may express gender in one way when at home with their family and in another when out with friends. A person may do a gender in a particular way when they are performing onstage and in another when they are living their daily lives. Onstage–offstage negotiations of gender are a fourth theme of this book.

Methodology

My research methodology is grounded in my training in ethnomusicology, a discipline that centers the relationships between culture and music and related performing arts such as dance and theater. As in anthropology, a discipline that has strongly influenced ethnomusicology, one important research methodology many scholars employ is ethnographic fieldwork, and specifically participant observation—spending time with a group of people (however defined) to learn from them by listening to what they have to say, observing what they do, and participating in activities with them, such as playing music or dancing. Although I focus on dance in this book, I believe it worth including that given my interest in both music and dance performance practice, I spent much of my time in Malang studying the playing techniques of several gamelan instruments, focusing on Malangan and east Javanese playing styles as well as studying east Javanese male- and female-style dances. I had two or more private lessons most weeks—each of which tended to be at least two hours in duration. In between lessons I practiced extensively alone, with a friend, or with groups of various sizes. Sometimes I joined practice sessions of other groups, and sometimes I organized practice sessions with the musicians in my primary gamelan teacher's group so that I could gain more experience playing or dancing with a fuller ensemble. With the help of my teachers, I also organized video and audio recording sessions to document the music and dance that my teachers were teaching me.

Lessons, practice sessions, and recording sessions provided not only invaluable experience in learning about how the music and dance forms worked, but also provided many opportunities for me to listen—and here I emphasize listen, and the intentionality of listening—to musicians and dancers as they shared their experiences as artists, their perspectives about the arts, their offstage lives, and more. I also conducted formal interviews with artists. Hanging out with my teachers and other artists provided additional rich opportunities to listen. I listened to people in the community in which I resided, including neighbors and people who became friends. Chit-chat with taxi drivers and mini-bus drivers were further opportunities to listen and to learn. My fieldwork included attending performances—where I was often provided explanations and commentary from my teachers, mentors, other artists, and members of the audience. Sometimes I recorded performances and watched them with my teachers. Watching performances together—either live or videotaped—gave me many opportunities to learn more from my teachers as they explained conventions, identified musical compositions, identified what performers were doing well and what they thought was not going so well or what they thought performers were not doing right. In this book I use the phrase "personal communication" in the in-text citations to indicate information I learned from listening to people in all of these ways.

I was also generously given opportunities to perform as a musician and dancer. These experiences taught me more about the arts, allowing me to experience the rush of performance in my own body, and provided opportunities for me to continue learning from my teachers as they offered advice for how to improve. Audiences received my performances very generously, encouraging me enthusiastically; many seemed appreciative that I would come all the way from the United States to learn about local traditions in Malang. For many, I believe, it was enjoyable to watch a foreign person perform local arts for the unusual aspect of it, and because on some level it showed that a Western person—and a US American in particular—was not as good as a local performer, which showed that Western culture and people were not inherently superior to Javanese/Indonesian people, in effect disrupting assumptions of Western superiority that have been internalized as a psychological impact of colonialism (Williams, 2001, p. 13; Sunardi, 2015, pp. xxiv–xxv; 2023, pp. 6–7).

While ethnographic research is the heart of my research methodology, I recognize that biases, implicit and explicit, are part and parcel of humans working together. For example, most of the artists I consulted over the course of my research in Malang were men as the professional traditional performing arts scene was largely male dominated. I have attempted to balance, at least somewhat, men's perspectives, voices, and experiences with those of women and *waria* I consulted, as well as my own perspectives as a woman (Sunardi, 2015, p. xxii). I also recognize that each individual—including me—has their own biases, opinions, perspectives, and so on that are shaped by multiple factors such as life experiences, personality, positionality, moment at which we interacted and what we were thinking about and feeling at that moment, and so on (Sunardi, 2015, p. xix). To present a range of perspectives and experiences, I offer portraits of six individual artists in this book, most of whom I consulted multiple times over the course of my fieldwork to build trust and to listen further, or in the case of a deceased artist, one I heard about on multiple occasions. And I strongly encourage you to read other analysts' work on Java, Indonesia, gender, other topics I address in this book, and other interests this book may spark to engage with still more perspectives, as my positionality (and personality) as a researcher also impacted my findings and the work that has resulted, including this book.

Author positionality

My own identity and perceptions of my identity were certainly factors as I worked with individuals in Malang, as were complicated power dynamics. I worked with a number of teachers as their student—they were the masters of the tradition and I was a novice. I was at their mercy in terms of what they chose to share (and not share) depending on what they felt I was ready to learn, what they wanted me to know to take back to the United States, what they felt was appropriate for me to know, and what they were thinking about on any given lesson day. At the same time, my status as a foreign researcher from the United States—I was in a PhD program during my fieldwork spanning 2005–2007 and on subsequent visits was a professor at a US university—held a lot of clout for many of the people with whom I worked. Given that I am a mixed-raced (Black, white, and a little Native American), brown-skinned woman married to a Javanese man, my skin color and marriage inclined people to think that I was like them to some degree. Many held their arms next to mine, noting the similarity in skin color, and saying things like "we are the same". Many assumed that I sincerely loved Javanese culture because I had married a Javanese person. Some expressed that I could understand them because I was from a historically marginalized group in the US as a Black/Brown person—that is, I could understand their plight as marginalized people in Indonesia due to their education level, class level, and/or regional identity as east Javanese culture is generally seen as less prestigious than central Javanese culture.

The maleness and femaleness many people in the community perceived in me due to my height and broad shoulders also led me to be mistaken for a *waria*. My activity performing a female-style dance that was associated with *waria* performers and the hellos I said to *waria* performers I saw on- and offstage reinforced assumptions that I was a *waria*, too. This gave me insights into how *waria* are perceived and treated, topics I discuss in the next chapter. (For more on my positionality as a "tall-broad-shouldered-foreign-but-brown female researcher", see Sunardi, 2015, pp. xxiii–xxix).

My path to Java

One question that I am often asked is how I came to be interested in Javanese culture in the first place. In some ways, the answer is quite simple—I became entranced by the sound of gamelan music during a music of Asia survey course I took as an undergraduate at the University of California, San Diego. It was unlike anything I had heard before and it captivated me. I had loved taking piano lessons as a child, playing clarinet in school concert and marching bands, later switching to mallets in marching band, and playing various saxophones in jazz band. Playing mallets led to an interest in percussion that I pursued in college and contributed to my fascination with gamelan—an orchestra comprised largely of percussion instruments. Right around the time I fell for gamelan, I was finalizing where to study abroad during my junior year (which I had long wanted to do) and decided to apply to the University of California study abroad program in Indonesia, which was based in Yogyakarta. I was accepted and during that program, 1997–1998, I had the opportunity to study gamelan and a little dance. I also met the man who would become my husband. The program was ended a little earlier than planned in May 1998 rather than July 1998 due to the political unrest surrounding the end of the authoritarian Suharto regime. After the political situation became more stable, I returned many times to visit my boyfriend, later fiancé, continuing to study gamelan and deepening my studies of central Javanese dance, particularly female-style dance. Aside from brief forays into ballet and tap as a child, I had not pursued much dance, preferring sports. With my boisterous, chatty, heart-on-my-sleeve demeanor, it was a new challenge to focus on central Javanese female-style dance with its controlled, subtle, and graceful movement and calm, unchanging, mask-like facial expression.

Fast forward to 2003, when I was in a PhD program in ethnomusicology at the University of California, Berkeley, I saw the internationally renowned master central Javanese dancer Didik Nini Thowok (b. 1954, Didik Hadiprayitno) perform *Beskalan Putri*, a female-style dance from Malang, in San Francisco (Sunardi, 2015, p. xxii). Didik, a celebrity in Indonesia, is a man who specializes in female-style dances (Janarto, 2005; Mrázek, 2005; Ross, 2005; Hughes-Freeland, 2008a). I had had the opportunity to meet him when I was living in central Java, and had the opportunity to participate as a musician in a performance project he directed that featured males, including him, performing female-style dance. (I decided to get into the cross-gender aspect and dressed as a male musician for the performance.) When I saw Didik perform *Beskalan Putri* in San Francisco, I was again taken—like when I was an undergraduate student and heard gamelan music for the first time. I had found my dissertation topic—or at least one of the dances that would be at the center of my dissertation research—and I plunged into the issue of gender.

During a preliminary trip to Malang in 2004, Didik helped introduce me to the community that became the base for my fieldwork. Once there, I learned about other east Javanese dances, including *Ngremo* and masked dances, and about east Javanese gamelan music and theater forms. In some ways, my previous studies of central Javanese gamelan and dance gave me a little bit of a head start on studying east Javanese gamelan and dance, but it also led to some mistaken assumptions about east Javanese music that I had to unlearn, as well as a certain touch in my playing and dancing that performers identified as central Javanese (Sunardi, 2010, pp. 99, 106, 118–119; 2017, pp. 62–63). I believe this contributed to my many conversations with performers about what made the music and dance I was studying east Javanese and Malangan in particular, which, as indicated, was critically important to them. My own interest in gender and performers' attention to the articulation of local identity through the arts has thus been at the center of much of my work in various manifestations, including this book.

Chapter summary

This chapter has offered an introduction to *Fashioning Femininities, Making Masculinities: Gender, Performance, and Lived Experience in Java, Indonesia*, including its focus on gender as a cultural construction that people continuously negotiate and ways we can understand how individuals negotiate gender through the performing arts and their lived experiences as artists in specific cultural contexts—in this case Malang in east Java. I have presented my analytical approaches to gender, including gender performativity—gender as an unstable cultural construct that people produce by "doing" gender in particular ways (Butler 1990; 1993; 1999)—and intersectionality—gender intersects with many other aspects of a person's identity, all of which are fluid and produced in and through complex webs of power

(Crenshaw, 1991; Nash, 2008; Cho, Crenshaw, and McCall, 2013, p. 795; see also Del Negro and Berger, 2004). I also build upon the concepts of gender pluralism (Peletz, 2006), female masculinity (Halberstam, 1998), male femininity (Boellstorff, 2004b; 2005b; 2007), and contingent gender (Blackwood, 2010).

My intent in this chapter has also been to make transparent that this book and its findings are products of my individual experiences and perspectives as a researcher and very much situated in my experiences conducting ethnographic fieldwork in Malang primarily spanning 2005 to 2007, with a prior visit to Malang in 2004 and subsequent visits, the most recent of which was in 2015 at the time of this writing. No less influential in the shaping of my work is my positionality as a mixed-race US American woman researcher, including my path to Java and east Javanese performing arts. I invite you to take this book for what it is and to seek out other perspectives. I am nonetheless excited to introduce you to individual dancers in the following two chapters. Through the stories they shared about their lives and experiences, as well as the perspectives they shared about the arts, we have the opportunity and privilege to explore themes of onstage–offstage gender negotiations, gender fluidity, gender pluralism, and spirituality.

Learning objectives

My hope is that by the time you finish this book, you will be able to:

1. Identify ways the performance of dance in Malang provides cultural space in which gender norms can be reinforced, subverted, challenged, navigated, and so on—sometimes all at the same time;

2. Provide examples of complex senses of gender that both push at and reinforce a culturally dominant heterosexual, male–female gender binary;

3. Explain how the cultural context of Malang informs individuals' negotiations of gender in the performing arts on- and offstage;

4. Apply theoretical and methodological approaches used in this book to the exploration of gender and performing arts traditions in various cultural and historical contexts; and

5. Build from the theoretical and methodological approaches used in this book to develop new approaches that are informed by the performing tradition(s) and cultural context(s) you are analyzing.

2
Male femininity on- and offstage

A man posing as another man's second wife to see how a first wife would react? The use of spiritual knowledge to embody femaleness through a male body? Insistence upon modeling respectable images of womanhood? These were some of the images that captured my attention as the dancers Djupri and Muliono, who lived as men, and Mama Samsu, who lived as a *waria* (a male who dresses and lives as female), shared aspects of their lives and careers.

Through their stories about their lived experiences in on- and offstage realms drawn from my earlier work (Sunardi, 2009; 2013; 2015), I show that while Djupri, Muliono, and Mama Samsu challenged assumptions in dominant Indonesian gender ideologies about what types of bodies could and should produce and embody femaleness as they produced male femininity, they also reinforced dominant representations of ideal womanhood through their onstage performances of traditional female-style dance, complicating the representation and cultural production of gender in Malang. I show, too, different ways they related to male femininity in offstage realms. As a reminder, the concept of male femininity was presented in the previous chapter and is femininity that is produced and embodied by males (Boellstorff; 2004b; 2005b, pp. 169, 171, 175; 2007, pp. 82, 99, 108; Sunardi, 2013, p. 141; 2015, p. 11; 2022, p. 290). In producing, embodying, and representing various gender identities—reinforcing gender pluralism—as they navigated expectations of gender and social pressures from the community, Djupri, Muliono, and Mama Samsu contributed to the production of east Javanese, and more specifically Malangan, place-based identities through the course of the mid-twentieth century and into the twenty-first.

It is my hope that by the end of this chapter you will be able to identify ways in which Djupri, Muliono, and Mama Samsu:

1.   Challenged and reinforced norms of gender and sexuality on- and offstage;

2.   Navigated gender and social pressures (including religious pressures) from the communities in which they lived; and

3.   Contributed to the production of local east Javanese identities through their lives and careers as artists.

Djupri: Gender fluidity on- and offstage

Djupri (b. 1939), who performed female and male-style dances over the course of his long career, was one of my most influential dance teachers. I studied the dances *Beskalan Putri* (*Beskalan* in the female style) and *Beskalan Lanang* (*Beskalan* in the male style) with him over the course of many months, going by motorbike—often taken by my husband or one of my other teachers—to his home in the village of Ngadireso in the sub-district of Poncokusuma multiple times a week for hours-long lessons (Figure 2 in Chapter 1). During lesson breaks and more formal interviews, Djupri shared stories about his life, including riveting ways he challenged gender norms on- and offstage in the 1950s and 1960s when he was frequently performing female-style dance. He continued to perform female roles, including female-style dance, in *ludruk* theater until 1993. *Ludruk* is a form of east Javanese theater that historically featured all male casts, with males performing both male and female roles. *Ludruk* troupes from Malang at the time of my fieldwork continued this practice for the most part. Djupri performed both male and female roles in *ludruk* between 1979 and 1993, and just male roles, including male-style dance, since 1993 (personal communication, Djupri, January 6, 2006).

I recognize that Djupri's stories were filtered through memory and shaped by the points he was making to me in 2005–2006— sometimes decades after their occurrence (Neuman, 1993, p. 276; Stoler with Strassler, 2002, p. 170; Zurbuchen, 2005, p. 7; Sunardi, 2015, pp. 25–28). I nonetheless value his recollections as evidence of gender fluidity, pluralism, and nonconformity in the 1950s, 1960s, and beyond—post-independence (post-1945) times when the Indonesian state was making an effort to shape masculinity and femininity in particular ways by mapping biological sex to gender in a one-to-one ratio and privileging heterosexuality, as outlined in the previous chapter (Blackwood, 2005, pp. 866, 869–871; 2007, pp. 185–188; Sunardi, 2009; 2013; 2015; 2022). That observational evidence from anthropologists Clifford Geertz's and James Peacock's fieldwork during the 1950s and 1960s in Java support Djupri's points, as do memories of other performers I consulted, indicates that the gender crossings

Djupri related were not isolated incidents. Djupri's memories of his experiences provide a window into ways one person embodied different gender identities and produced contingent senses of gender. Impressed by the ways Djupri moved between femaleness and maleness depending on the dance he was teaching me, I was fascinated by the ways he described his gender fluidity in the past, including internally, externally, as well as onstage and offstage (Sunardi, 2009, pp. 463–468; 2015, pp. 63–93).

Use of *ilmu* (spiritual knowledge)

On an internal level, Djupri used *ilmu* (spiritual knowledge, often of a secretive nature) to embody femaleness. In talking about his experiences performing female roles including *Ngremo Putri* (*Ngremo* in the female style) for *ludruk*, which he did from 1958 to 1993, Djupri explained that he could dance and feel like a woman on stage because of his *ilmu*, which he took from a heavenly nymph (*dewi widadari*). Responding to my question about whether he felt like a real woman when dancing *Ngremo Putri*, he said yes, explaining that his transformation was so complete that,

> [M]y feeling was that, with women, it was yeah, rather, like a feeling of hate … in fact hate. My favorites were instead handsome people [men]. That was when … performing *ludruk*, though, yeah. I liked wome- handsome men, instead I yeah, yes, I liked them. Indeed. A recollection of *ludruk*.
>
> [P]erasaan saya itu, dengan orang wanita, itu ya, agak, seperti rasa benci itu … malah benci. Senangannya malah orang yang ganteng-ganteng itu. Itu kalau … waktu ludrukan lho ya. Dengan orang wanit- orang pria yang

ganteng itu malah saya iya, ya senang. Memang. Kenangan ludruk. (personal communication, Djupri, January 6, 2006)

In talking about his preference for and attraction to handsome men (while in the mindset of a female), Djupri reinforced heterosexual norms even as he articulated what could also be understood as a homosexual desire.

At the same time, he distanced feelings of hating women and preferring handsome men from his genuine self by specifying that it was his use of *ilmu* for the purpose and moment of performance that made him feel this way. He also clarified that he was entered by a heavenly nymph, that is, a spirit, when performing *Ngremo Putri*. In other words, feeling like a woman in the sense of being attracted to men and repulsed by women was temporary, contingent on the context of performance, and a result of being entered by a feminine spirit (Sunardi, 2009, p. 464; 2015, pp. 79–80). His slippage between liking women vs. men toward the end of the quote is also noteworthy as on some level it further shows the fluidity of his sexual desire as he moved in and out of performing *Ngremo Putri*, which I understand as another manifestation of gender fluidity as he moved between the femaleness of the performed persona and the maleness of his own self.

Reinforcing heterosexual norms, he also described using *ilmu* when performing male-style dance to look handsome and attractive to women, giving the example of using *ilmu* from the god Arjuna when performing *Ngremo Lanang* (*Ngremo* in the male style), and being entered by Arjuna (Sunardi, 2015, p. 187n9). Using *ilmu* was thus one strategy Djupri employed to perform femaleness and maleness, as well as to move between femaleness and maleness—that is, to move from the maleness of his own self to the femaleness he embodied on stage, and to move from the femaleness of female-style dances to the maleness of male-style dances.

Contradictory expectations

As a male who performed female-style dance, Djupri also had to contend with contradictory expectations about gender, including social needs and desires for male femininity despite dominant expectations that mapped masculinity to male bodies and femininity to female bodies. For example, when audiences knew that a performer who was performing female-style dance or performing as a female singer-dancer was male, they could respond to the performer's femaleness more freely than would be socially acceptable with a woman or girl. Djupri said that when he was performing as an itinerant female singer-dancer, or *andhong*, in the mid-1950s to early 1960s, people in Malang knew that he was male because they knew him personally. When Djupri performed as an *andhong*, he shared with pride in his voice, viewers preferred him to a female because they could dance more freely with him and even kiss him, behaviors that social norms prevented them from indulging in if the dancer were a woman or girl (personal communication, June 15, 2006).

In the *andhong* tradition, professional female performers sing and dance for audience members who pay to request a song. *Andhong* was the term for both the professional dancer and the group. A group usually included one or two dancers, who were usually women, although, as Djupri's experience indicates, male dancers also dressed as females. The person who requests a song also dances with the professional dancer. As itinerant performers, *andhong* wandered from village to village looking for places to perform. According to performers I talked to, the *andhong* tradition was practiced from the early twentieth century until about 1965, although traditions in which female entertainers sing and dance for people who request songs very much continue to the present in other forms such as *tayub* dance events, discussed in the next chapter (personal communication, Kusnadi, November 17, 2005; Supatman, December 6, 2005; Madya, December 17, 2005; Tri Wahyuningtyas, December 17, 2005; Chattam Amat Redjo, April 14, 2006; Panoto, May 16, 2006; Sutanu, June 7, 2006; Djupri, June 15, 2006; Asbari, June 29, 2006; Timan, July 4, 2006; and Satupah, July 7, 2006). The anthropologist Clifford Geertz also observed such groups in the 1950s; he referred to the dancers as *klèdek* or *tandhak*. He reported that such groups included as many as two or three dancers (1960, pp. 296–300).

Despite social norms that may have inhibited similar indulgences with female performers, the sexual desires for Djupri—and the acting upon those desires—when he was dressed as a female while known to be male suggests sexual desire specifically for male femininity and for gender fluidity. On one level, such desires reinforce heterosexual desire promulgated as normative in dominant gender ideologies because the dancer is dressed as female, and viewers would be interacting with what they were allowing themselves to perceive as a woman or girl, at least in the moment of performance. On another level, such desires express a same-sex desire when viewers knew that Djupri was a male cross-dressed as a female. In some cases, by Djupri's own account explored below, he did also pass as female.

Men's obsession with male singer-dancers dressed as females, and the use of esoteric forces, was not unique to Djupri's experience in the 1950s and 1960s. Clifford Geertz and James Peacock observed similar kinds of reactions among audiences in their research on *ludruk*. Geertz, describing *ludruk* in the early 1950s in the town of Modjukuto (a pseudonym), writes that the males who performed female roles activated a sense of wonder (1960, p. 295). Peacock also found in his research on *ludruk* theater in Surabaya during the 1960s that sometimes male audience members became so sexually drawn to a male performing a female role that the audience member would try "to marry" the performer, and that it was believed that performers had "magical power" to arouse such desires (Peacock, 1978, p. 218; Sunardi, 2015, pp. 77–78). Speaking to further back in the past, the drummer Sutanu (1935–2008) recalled that in the 1940s and 1950s, men often fell in love with males who performed female roles in *ludruk* and that performers used magic so that audiences would fall in love with them; he and the drummer Kusnadi (1944–2016)—my principle gamelan teacher in Malang—said that sometimes a man would call a particular performer his wife and become jealous if the performer was approached by another man (personal communication, June 7, 2006).

Onstage–offstage implications

Sexual and romantic desires for males who performed female roles onstage had offstage implications. Speaking further to his ability to sexually arouse those who saw him perform female-style dance, Djupri recounted an instance when a man—a retired military officer who had seen Djupri perform at an event for retired military officers–became so obsessed after seeing him perform that he followed Djupri to Djupri's home and other gigs. Djupri recalled this retired officer as being "crazy" (*gila*) and forgetting about his own family (personal communication, June 15, 2006).

Djupri himself took the femaleness he performed as a dancer into his daily life in several ways when he was young and frequently performing female-style dance, embodying and producing male femininity in different realms of culture. Sometimes doing so was a practical matter. For example, recalling his activities in the 1960s, Djupri talked about items he used to transform his appearance, including wigs with real hair that could be glued on to the head and used to make a large bun. Specifying that these wigs were from Japan, he implied their high quality and expense as well as his intentionality and care to look like he naturally had long hair. He explained that sometimes he kept the wig on in his offstage daily life because it was easier than removing and reattaching it every day (personal communication, June 15, 2006; Sunardi, 2009, p. 464; 2015, pp. 79–80).

Although Djupri couched his wearing of the wig offstage in terms of practicality, he was nonetheless subverting dominant ideologies of gender and resisting social pressures to conform to dominant ideologies of manhood. James Peacock points to the impact that dominant discourses had on performers' behavior and lifestyles in 1960s Surabaya, noting that after the Indonesian revolution (1945–1949), it was considered more progressive and modern for males who performed female roles to live as men. He cites two who had cut their long hair because of "progress", which was distressing because, as a natural part of the body, long hair was a special symbol of a male performer's commitment to womanhood offstage as well as on (1987, p. 207). They were discouraged from taking gender transgression into their daily lives as they were encouraged to be modern, Indonesian men—to have short hair, wear pants, and be heads of households (Peacock, 1987, pp. 206–207; see also Boellstorff, 2007, pp. 86–87; Sunardi, 2015, pp. 64–65). In other words, the performers' male femininity was expected to be contingent, limited to the context of performance. As we have seen, though, sexual desires for offstage male femininity were aroused and sometimes acted upon. In leaving his wig on in between performances, Djupri undermined dominant norms and expectations as he produced and embodied male femininity on- as well as offstage.

Further taking gender transgression into his daily life, Djupri recounted proudly that he was able to fool people into believing that he was a girl when in female attire. On one occasion in about 1966 or 1967, a man who had seen Djupri perform female-style dance asked him to remain in female dress and pose as his second wife so that the man could see how his current wife would react. Djupri and this man challenged the mapping of femininity to female bodies in dominant Indonesian discourses. While they reinforced the appearance of a heterosexual relationship, they were enacting a same-sex relationship, albeit temporarily (and Djupri gave no indication that it was sexually consummated). Djupri did not specify how long he posed as the man's second wife, but it was long enough to wear women's clothes in public and go to a market—the idea being that he would shop and the first wife would cook as a test to see if the first wife could get along with a second wife as they divided the labor of running a household (personal communication, June 15, 2006).

Highlighting his ability to pass as a girl and trick people about his identity, Djupri related that his uncle, who had been looking for Djupri, saw him at the market when Djupri was dressed in women's clothes, uncertain whether it was actually Djupri. The uncle followed him around the market, but it was not until Djupri said hello to him that his uncle recognized him. The uncle followed Djupri to the man's house. Djupri went in, put the vegetables he had bought away in the kitchen, and then went into a room to change clothes. He remembered still having glue on his forehead from the wig when he came out to where his uncle was waiting in the front room with the man's wife. She kept looking at Djupri and said something about who was this and why did he look like the girl her husband had brought home? The situation was clarified and Djupri went home with his uncle (personal communication, June 15, 2006). That Djupri exuded pride and pleasure in his tone of voice and smiles as he shared these memories of being able to pass so convincingly as a female in daily life suggests his delight in subverting dominant gender norms and expectations through cross-gender performance offstage as well as on.

Performance provided cultural space for gender transgression that bled into daily life for other individuals in the 1960s, providing a bigger picture of gender pluralism in Java during this time period. Observing masked dance in Malang in 1963, the historian Onghokham mentions the role of a *waria* as an artistic aid to a troupe leader (1972, p. 119). That this person was a "well-situated villager" indicates that this individual, in some ways at least, did not occupy a completely marginalized position within the community (Onghokham, 1972, p. 119). Despite the social pressures James Peacock identified for males who performed female roles to live as men in Surabaya, he also writes that nearly all of the males who performed as females he consulted in the early 1960s embodied femininity in their offstage lives, refusing to conform to dominant expectations and social pressures: they wore women's clothes when at home and sometimes out in public and worked jobs associated with women such as tailoring women's clothing. Many, however, had to deal with their "parents' discomfort and strangers' taunts" (Peacock, 1987, p. 207; Sunardi, 2015, pp. 65–66).

A body suit

Speaking to onstage–offstage gender transgression when talking about the tricks of the trade that he and other *ludruk* performers used to look as convincingly female as possible when performing, Djupri talked about the use of a type of body suit (Sunardi, 2009, pp. 463–464; 2015, pp. 80–81). This suit, he related, was also from Japan (like his wig)—again implying its expense and high quality, as well as the economic investment to look as female as possible on the part of a performer who purchased one. He described the body suit as a sort of outer skin complete with pores that made it look more realistic and allowed the wearer's skin to breathe. It also featured body hair and padding for breasts, hips, and buttocks. The suits came in different colors and models; his covered his upper arms and thighs, and went up the neck with padding to smooth over an Adam's apple. Some, which were more expensive, covered the entire arm and leg. Some also went up the face (personal communication, Djupri, June 15, 2006).

Overcoming his initial shyness with laughs and smiles as he talked to me—his female student in a daughterly relation to him—and my husband, whose presence likely made him feel more at liberty to discuss sexual matters, Djupri explained that the body suit made the genital area look convincingly female as well. Not only was the front of the crotch area smoothed over, a pocket was included to contain a man's genitals. The suit also contained a hole and pubic hair designed to resemble female genitalia. Referring to the use of this suit in private activity, he said that a man could have sex without the suit being taken off, reporting that it was said that sex was more pleasurable with the suit than with a female. He was quick to restate that that was what people said, emphasizing that he did not really know because he had never done this (personal communication, June 15, 2006).

Djupri's emphasis that he had never used the body suit in offstage sexual encounters was one way that despite his gender fluidity in on- and offstage realms, he asserted that he lived as a man. He introduced me to his wife and grown children when they were at his home, thereby positioning himself as a husband and father, as heterosexual, and as household head. He also distanced himself from a *waria* identity by expressing an ambivalent attitude toward *waria*. On the one hand, he linked *waria* to a form of magic that had connections to the sacred. He said that because of *ilmu*, the spirit or soul (*kejiwaan*) of a man was a woman's spirit or soul (*jiwa wanita*). On the other hand, he said that *waria's ilmu* was not the person's own, implying that it was bought from sorcerers, and thus assumed to be temporary and less valued in Java than *ilmu* gained via spiritual pursuits and ascetic practices (Keeler, 1987, p. 236; Sunardi, 2015, pp. 147, 191n10; in press). He underscored that he did not want that kind of *ilmu* (personal communication, January 6, 2006).

Familial and religious pressures

Identifying familial and religious pressures to conform to dominant ideologies of gender, Djupri referenced his grandmother's religiously inspired instruction to become a woman only when he performed, but not in daily life because God had made him a man. While Djupri's grandmother sanctioned his gender nonconformity despite some aspects of dominant religious ideology—such as not to cross-dress at all—she insisted that he conform to others—such as not to cross-dress in his offstage life. This suggests her own conflicted relationship with the religious convictions circulating in their community, the limits of gender transgression she approved, and her concern for Djupri to be socially accepted, particularly as she may have heard of Djupri's activities posing as a female offstage or men who had fallen for him following him around (Sunardi, 2015, p. 88).

Djupri continued to hold himself to high standards of being able to pass as female in his performances of female-style dance to the point that he declined my requests to videotape him performing *Beskalan Putri*. He believed he was no longer slim, young, pretty (when in costume with makeup), or graceful enough, and he felt stiff because he had not performed female-style dance for over ten years at the time I made the requests (personal communication, Djupri, December 1, 2005; January 6, 2006; March 27, 2006; Sunardi, 2015, p. 88). He did let me document him performing the male-style dances *Ngremo Lanang* and *Beskalan Lanang*, and he let me record him playing the drum for *Beskalan Putri*. Despite his reluctance to perform female-style dance at the time of my fieldwork, his lived experiences including his activities as an artist from the 1950s, 1960s, and into the 1990s point to ways he contributed to the production of male femininity and what it meant to be male and female in different ways in the Malang area, thereby contributing to the production of local culture—including performing arts—and identity through his gender fluidity and articulations of gender pluralism. I wonder to what extent, in teaching me *Beskalan Putri* in the early 2000s, he was continuing to produce male femininity as he taught me to embody and perform femaleness.

Muliono: Navigating gender

Muliono (b. 1976–1977?), or Mul for short, entranced me with his powerful performances of strong male-style masked dance. I was astonished, then, to learn from him that he used to perform female characters in masked dance drama when he was younger and smaller in build. I was delightfully shocked that a man that I had thought of as so masculine and manly—onstage as well as offstage—had contributed to the production of male femininity. As we saw with Djupri, Muliono's performances of femaleness onstage had offstage implications, and like Djupri, Muliono chose ultimately to live as a man. Muliono, however, drew a clearer line between his onstage performance of femininity and the masculinity of his offstage self (Sunardi, 2015, pp. 67–70).

Contingent female masculinity

Muliono emphasized that his embodiment of femininity was contingent on the context of performance. He performed female characters out of necessity to the performance, he explained, because female dancers in his community at that time (likely the 1980s and into the early 1990s) were shy about performing masked dance, and because the other male masked dancers could not perform female-style dance (personal communication, January 3, 2006). Distancing the femininity he projected onstage from his own character, demeanor, internal feelings and sense of self, he talked about embodying femaleness through his ability and skill as a dancer. He specified that he became "female" through the dance movement, saying that it had to be supple, like a woman, and through the costume. That masks were used, I believe, also helped him not only to take on and articulate the femininity of the female character he was portraying for the performance, but also to distance his own self from femaleness as he was literally putting on the face of a character he was portraying. Reiterating the contingency of the femininity he was performing, he explained that he felt the coquettishness of the female character he was dancing when he came out on to the stage, but the feeling of becoming a woman disappeared when he was finished performing (personal communication, Muliono, January 3, 2006). In other words, offstage he felt like himself—male.

Another strategy Mul used to perform female characters, like Djupri, was spiritual. In Mul's case, the way he talked about using spiritual practices reinforced the contingency of his embodiment of femaleness and was a way of distancing the femaleness from his own self as a male. For example, he asked for a mantra or magic words from his teacher, which he likened to meditating, so that the character could enter. He said that he truly felt like the female character he was portraying to the point of not remembering dancing—indicating that he was in a trancelike state as a spirit possessed his body. His performances of femaleness impacted audiences, as he recalled that after he performed, his friends asked with amazement, "How was it that you were like a real woman?" (personal communication, January 3, 2006). The femaleness he embodied was not his own, he implied, but that of an outside entity, as we also saw with Djupri. Being entered by a character or spirit gave Mul—and others—a way to make sense of his gender identity as male even as he had the ability to perform femaleness so convincingly. Embodying a character or spirit so completely also reinforced his ability as a dancer as many artists in different regions of Java value performances given by dancers believed to be entered in these ways and serve as vessels for spiritual beings, characters, spiritual power, and/or *ilmu* (Foley, 1985, p. 36; Schrieber, 1991, p. 26; Weiss, 2003, pp. 37, 42; Sunardi, 2015, p. 68; in press).

While Mul separated his onstage and offstage embodiments of gender, his cultural work producing male femininity nonetheless was significant as it still undermined the mapping of male bodies to masculinity and female bodies to femininity in dominant discourses, still ultimately showing gender to be fluid, crossable, and plural. He spoke to further crossings of gender within one performance, relating that he performed a female role and then played the male character Gunung Sari (personal communication, January 3, 2006). Such a transformation likely entailed a costume change, a change in masks, as well as a change in demeanor—that is, a sartorial and character-based gender crossing. Given the spiritual dimensions discussed above, it may have also entailed allowing the spirit of the female character to leave his body and the spirit of a male one to enter. Interestingly, Gunung Sari is a male character with feminine aspects. The dance *Gunung Sari*, which presents the character of Gunung Sari, incorporates what dancers recognize as male and female movement styles, making *Gunung Sari* an interesting representation of masculinity imbued with femininity, which I analyze in more depth elsewhere (Sunardi, 2020).

Moving away from female roles

Muliono related how he moved away from performing female roles as he matured into a man and assumed the roles of husband and household head, thus conforming to dominant Indonesian expectations of being a man that were reinforced in his local community and family. One of the reasons he moved away from performing female roles, it seemed, was because in his offstage life he became associated with the femaleness of the character(s) he was portraying. He recalled that his friends in one neighborhood often jokingly called him "sister/miss" (*mbak*) (personal communication, January 3, 2006). Muliono's association with femaleness offstage corroborates Karen Elizabeth Schrieber's findings that masked dancers tend to become connected to the spirit associated with a mask (1991, p. 26). Over time, Muliono did not want to be associated with the femininity of the female characters he was portraying—perhaps the joking from his friends felt like taunting—and he turned his attention to male roles.

Muliono explained that he did not want to perform female roles after he married (in about 1995) in part because his wife Ning (a pseudonym) joined the masked dance group in his hamlet of Dampul and performed those roles. One implication is that since a woman was available and trained to perform female roles, he was no longer needed in that capacity. Furthermore, since performed characters tended to be associated with a performer's lived identity, if both he and his wife performed female roles in the same troupe, it could ultimately emasculate him as a husband, father (or future father), and household head in relation to his wife. On some level it could also undermine perceptions of a heterosexual relationship between him and his wife by sparking homoerotic imaginations.

Muliono spoke further about concerns pertaining to the perceptions of his masculinity in relation to his marriage—again, a time when he was expected to conform to dominant expectations of being a man. Prior to his marriage, he explained, he often performed female roles, although up in the Tengger mountains, which was away from his home community. He did not want to perform female roles in his home area because Ning's parents were there, and he was *malu*—an Indonesian word that can be roughly translated as shy or embarrassed—in front of them, especially Ning's father. He said that her parents liked it when he performed *Klana* (personal communication, January 3, 2006). It is important to understand that *Klana* is a strong male-style masked dance, and as such, features a wide stance, high arm positions, and large movement volumes (as compared to *Gunung Sari* with its narrower stance, lower arm positions and feminine aspects) (Figures 6 and 7). Muliono thus felt encouraged to embody a "manly" (hypermasculine, one might say) sense of masculinity, perhaps a gendered quality parents-in-law or potential parents-in-law would tend to find more appealing than feminine qualities in a son-in-law or potential son-in-law. Mul, too, may have wished to demonstrate that he was manly and capable, or had the potential, of being a worthy husband, household head, and father.

Figure 6. A dancer performs the masked dance *Klana*. Photograph taken by Mr. Sunardi, 2009.

Figure 7. A dancer performs the masked dance *Gunung Sari*. The
dancer is in a kneeling position, but the lower arm position and
smaller movement volume compared to *Klana* in Figure 6 can be seen.
Photograph by Mr. Sunardi, 2006.

In other contexts, too, Mul reinforced and articulated his hetero-sexual, "manly" sense of masculinity. He explained that he did not want to perform female roles at a particular art center because he had lots of female friends there (personal communication, Muliono, January 3, 2006). In short, when he wished to be per-ceived as a heterosexual, "manly" male, he avoided performing female-style dance.

Muliono is not the only male performer who avoided performing female roles in his home community out of concerns that doing so would compromise perceptions of his manliness. The anthro-pologist Ward Keeler gives an example of a Javanese man who performed the comic maidservant role in *ketoprak*, a type of cen-tral Javanese theater. After this man became a grandfather, he no longer wished to perform near his home because "he would feel *isin* [Javanese for shy, embarrassed] to be seen performing by his own neighbors and kin" (Keeler, 1983, p. 163). In addition to concerns about being seen performing a comic role, he may have been concerned that his embodiment of femaleness would compromise his status and reputation as a senior, male figure in his community whose seniority rested in part on the perception of his grandfatherhood, and by extension, his fatherhood and heterosexuality.

Mul and the *ketoprak* actor's concerns contrast with Djupri's pride in the ways he could fool people on- and offstage. Djupri, too, however, did ultimately live as a man in his offstage life and did also specify ways his transformations to femaleness were contingent, temporary, and done for specific reasons, such as to perform (and earn a livelihood), the practicalities of leaving on a difficult-to-remove wig in between performances, and because he was asked to pose as a second wife. These examples contrast with the example of Mama Samsu, introduced next, who embodied femaleness onstage and confidently lived as a *waria*.

Mama Samsu: Female masculinity and respectability politics

Mama Samsu (Samsuarto, 1955–2018) was an important figure in the *ludruk* and *waria* communities in Malang at the time of my fieldwork (Sunardi, 2009, pp. 477–478, 482–483; 2013, pp. 154–157; 2015, pp. 66–67, 72–75, 91). She began to study the arts as a child and actively performed in *ludruk* from 1978–1991. I use female pronouns when referring to Mama Samsu since she went by the feminine term of address "mama". In the Indonesian language, pronouns are not gendered, although terms of address are. In addition to performing, Mama Samsu worked as a beautician and as a seamstress. At the time I interviewed her in 2006 she owned a successful salon and boutique in the city of Malang. She mentored many younger *waria* performers and members of the *waria* community in general. She and her long-term partner Totok Suprapto offered critical insights into *waria*'s experiences and she also expressed the importance of *waria* taking it upon themselves to present a positive image of themselves through their work and lifestyles so that people in the community would value them and their work.

I view such activism in a marginalized community through the lens of respectability politics or the politics of respectability. As developed in African American studies, this lens has been used to analyze ways, rationales, and implications of African

Americans as members of a marginalized group intentionally adopting senses of ideal, respectable behavior, manners, morals, styles of dress, and other ways of being associated with hegemonic American culture rooted in middle- and upper-class Euro-American values and norms as a means of advancing African American communities in part by proving to dominant society and to themselves that they, too, deserve respect, equality, and fair treatment (Higginbotham, 1993, pp. 14–15, 185–229; White, 2001, pp. 14, 36–37; Rabaka, 2012, pp. 42–43, 53–54, 62; Brown, 2020, pp. 2–4, 30, 69; Jefferson, 2023, pp. 1449, 1451, 1453). Similarly, Mama Samsu as a member of the *waria* community, a marginalized group in Java, spoke to ways *waria* needed to present a respectable image of themselves—to show that they are polite, well-mannered, and do good work—in order to be valued and ultimately accepted.

Visibility of *waria*

Although the Indonesian government reinforced heterosexuality and men's roles as household heads of nuclear families, males who dressed and lived as female have insisted on their visibility and acceptance both socially and politically since the 1970s (Boellstorff, 2004b; 2005b, pp. 56–57; 2007), and have been, to a certain extent, tolerated and supported by the government. The culturally sensitive term many used to identify themselves at the time of my fieldwork, *waria*—a composite of the Indonesian words for woman (**wa**nita) and man (*p***ria**)—is a term that dates from a 1978 government dictate (Boellstorff, 2007, p. 83; Sunardi, 2015, pp. 65–67). Furthermore, *waria* have received recognition and support from local governments since the second half of the 1960s (Oetomo, 2000, p. 51).

The anthropologist Tom Boellstorff notes that since the mid-1960s, *waria* have been working to increase their visibility and social acceptance by more openly wearing women's clothes and establishing themselves in salon work (2004b; 2007, pp. 86–87). According to Mama Samsu and Totok, *waria* started to have the confidence to live openly since the 1970s as more *waria* started to appear nationally and internationally in events such as competitions in makeup, beauty, and fashion (personal communication, May 9 and 16, 2006). Boellstorff observes a "shift around 1980, when some people began identifying as *waria* on an ongoing basis in public (as opposed to more circumscribed contexts like theatrical performances)" (2005b, p. 56). Indicative of increased visibility, a *waria* was a contender for mayor in the city of Malang in 2003 (Boellstorff, 2004b, p. 187n19; 2007, p. 226 n15).

Work in the beauty industry has been part of *waria*'s larger efforts and social activism to negotiate cultural and economic space more prominently. Mama Samsu explained that these kinds of occupations appeal to *waria* because they can dress up and wear makeup daily. In other words, these occupations allowed *waria* to remain visible as *waria* in their working worlds, contributing to the visibility of *waria* in society more broadly (Boellstorff, 2005b, p. 143). These careers also provided an important source of income. Mama Samsu trained many *ludruk* performers who were *waria* as seamstresses and makeup artists so that they could supplement their earnings from performing and enter professions with steadier incomes—particularly as they aged and became less able to rely on their physical beauty. Samsu indicated that *waria* can make positive contributions to their communities and improve their image through good work in the beauty industry (personal communication, May 9 and 16, 2006). She voiced the responsibility that many Indonesian gay male, lesbian, and *waria* individuals have taken toward their acceptance in society by doing good deeds—that is, "something 'positive' (*positip*)" (Boellstorff, 2005b, p. 212).

I noticed *waria*'s visibility during my fieldwork and subsequent visits to Malang spanning 2005 to 2015. I saw *waria* working in salons, performing in *ludruk* shows, attending *ludruk* performances, and out and about in public. I noticed representations of *waria* on television, corroborating the visibility in mass media that other analysts have noted (Boellstorff, 2007, p. 88; Murtagh, 2011, pp. 392–393n3). Some *ludruk* performers identified openly as *waria* and went by feminine terms of address such as mama (*mama*), miss/sister (*mbak*), or missus (*nyonya*) (see also Pawestri, 2006, pp. 101–109), and as highlighted by Tjundomanik Tjatur Pawestri, some went by feminine names (ibid., p. 101).

Struggles for gender inclusive social acceptance

Tolerance and visibility, however, were not synonymous with acceptance, and local pressures, including familial and religious, reinforced dominant, official ideologies pushing males to live as "manly" men (Oetomo, 2000, p. 49; Boellstorff, 2005b, pp. 11–12, 57; 2007, pp. 78–113; Murtagh, 2011, pp. 392–393n3). Mama Samu and Totok talked about *waria*'s struggles to be accepted by their families and communities, as did the *waria* consulted by Tom Boellstorff (2004b; 2007). In villages, Mama Samsu said, where people tend to be more close-minded than in cities, the families of males with what she and Totok identified as women's hearts often force them to live as men and marry women, sometimes with tragic consequences. While she recognized that people in the city tended to be more tolerant and that *waria*'s work in makeup, fashion, and performance was appreciated, even in the city, not all males with women's hearts who were active in *ludruk* (or in general) had the confidence to live openly as *waria*.

For males who had women's hearts but did not live openly as *waria*, performance was a critically important cultural space in which to embody womanhood, even if just for the duration of the performance (personal communication, Mama Samsu and Totok, May 9, 2006). That is, some males with women's hearts felt safe expressing womanhood in the context of performance— another example of contingent male femininity—and lived their daily lives as men. Exuding an impressive and contagious confidence (I can understand her impact as a mentor), Mama Samsu said that she, however, does not feel freer on stage than in daily life because she already feels free to wear whatever she wants. She does not care what people say.

This confidence—and courage—has not come without cost. Discussing experiences with discrimination, Mama Samsu related that when she was in college her BA thesis was failed because she dressed like a woman. Persisting, she graduated in 1982. She also experienced discrimination from people on religious grounds, explaining that some orthodox Muslims believed that having one's makeup done by a *waria* beautician was filthy (personal communication, May 9 and 16, 2006). Countering religiously inspired discriminatory discourses, she justified her male femininity in her day-to-day life by posing the question of who was judging, humans or God, answering that God is the one to judge, and that everyone is God's creation. Referring to many *waria*'s and *ludruk* performers' experiences of being forced to live as men and marry women, but unable to satisfy their wives (implying sexually), Mama Samsu said that they cannot help it because they were made like that by God (personal communication, May 9, 2006). In other words, God made some males feminine and sexually desire male partners, not females.

Responding to my question about her religion, Mama Samsu explained that at one time she and Totok got into an argument about religion. She questioned why one had to approach God through Islam, articulating her belief in a supreme God while also expressing reservation about choosing Islam as the way to practice monotheism. She explained that:

> Pak Tot and I got into an argument in the past—oh, what year was that? Pak Tot entered Islam. Go ahead, [I said,] enter Islam, [but] approaching God does not [have to be] through Islam. As for me, every night that I can't sleep, yes, I ask God—after all the one who made me is God, right? If I feel that I am dirty, I bathe until I am clean and change into a clean shirt. Then I pray, God, I'm asking for this and this, what way is the path? Like that, right?
>
> *[S]ama Pak Tot dulu kemarin—tahun berapa itu ya—bertongkar sama-sama Pak Tot itu. Pak Tot itu ke, masuk Islam, lho silakan, masuk Islam, pendekatan dengan Tuhan itu nggak melalui Islam. Saya itu setiap malam ndak bisa tidurnya minta kepada Tuhan, o yang, yang membuat saya*

kan Tuhan. Saya kalau merasakan saya itu kotor gitu, ya,
mandi bersih gitu, ya wis, ganti baju bersih. Terus berdoa,
Tuhan saya minta gini, gini, jalannya gi mana. Kan gitu, ya?
(personal communication, Samsuarto, May 9, 2006)

Mama Samsu decided, however, to become Muslim with Totok
and they went to an Islamic boarding school, consulting an
Islamic teacher. Totok ended up distancing himself from Mama
Samsu, which led to their temporary breakup. Relating their
reunification, she explained that:

> In the end he got sick, asked someone for help, and I was
> asked to pick him up. Now, the one to judge is God, not
> those people.
>
> *Akhirnya sakit, sakit minta tolong orang gitu saya suruh*
> *jemput, gitu. Sekarang yang nilai Tuhan, bukan orang itu.*
> (personal communication, Samsuarto, May 9, 2006)

In explaining that when Totok became ill and that Mama Samsu
was the one who was called to pick him up, she implied that
Totok needed to be with her as his true love—he literally could
not be healthy without her. She also insisted on gender inclusivity through religious discourse by emphasizing that God is the
one to judge, not humans.

Mama Samsu's insistence on inclusivity in Islam has been ech-
oed by members of Indonesia's gay and lesbian communities.
According to Tom Boellstorff, while some males who identified as gay did find being homosexual a sin, the predominant
view Boellstorff found among gay men was that being gay was
either not sinful or "a minor sin easily forgiven by God" (2005a,
p. 580; 2005b, p. 183; 2007, p. 151). Many of the gay Muslim men

Boellstorff talked to referenced ultimate judgment by God, as did Mama Samsu. Also in the same vein as Mama Samsu, many determined that they were not sinning because God made them homosexual (Boellstorff, 2005a, p. 580; 2005b, p. 183; 2007, p. 151). The female Muslim homosexual people interviewed by the anthropologist Evelyn Blackwood recognized "that according to Islam homosexuality is a sin, but they find their own accommodations between their religious beliefs and their desires" (2010, pp. 15, 94). By making sense of Islam in their own ways to legitimize and include gender identities and sexual desires that were nonnormative by the standards of dominant Indonesian (and Islamic) gender ideology—as did Djupri and his grandmother to a certain extent—individuals such as Mama Samsu, Totok, those consulted by Boellstorff, and those consulted by Blackwood were contributing to the spectrum of beliefs, practices, and attitudes that comprise Islam in Java (Daniels, 2009).

Although Mama Samsu made sense of religion in her own way, she also recognized the importance of respect for the context, as when serving as a beautician for a wedding. She noted that when she goes to a mosque, she makes the effort to wear a headscarf. She also said that she wears appropriate attire when she goes to a church (personal communication, May 9, 2006). Mama Samsu's decision to wear women's attire to mosques is also significant because the issue of what waria should "wear when praying as Muslims" (Oetomo, 2000, p. 54)—male attire because they are male-bodied or were assigned male at birth, or female attire because they live as female—was unresolved within waria communities (Oetomo, 2000, pp. 54–55). By specifying women's attire (a headscarf) to go to mosques (although not necessarily specifying to pray), Mama Samsu insisted that Muslim society recognize the femininity with which she identified. Moreover, she provided an example to other *waria* who felt similarly about their femininity, while also demonstrating her own respectability. In light of the anthropologist Suzanne Brenner's point that, through veiling, some women in Java "refashion themselves to fit their image of modern Islamic womanhood" (1996, p. 691), Mama Samsu's decision to wear a veil also suggests that she was asserting a sense of modernity as she asserted her femininity.

Propriety

In talking about her propriety, piety, and long-term relationship with Totok (her partner of over 20 years at the time of my interviews with her), Mama Samsu implicitly countered negative assumptions about *waria*'s promiscuity and availability as prostitutes. Such assumptions contributed to teasing, taunting, sexual harassment, and belittlement that many *waria* endured as well as isolation, ambivalence, avoidance, and criticism. For example, because most performers knew that many *ludruk* performers who performed female roles at the time of my fieldwork lived as *waria*, their gender transgression in their daily lives was imagined when they were seen performing. One performer explained that he enjoys watching those who perform female roles in *ludruk* performances, including those who were *waria*. At the same time, he was afraid of *waria* and did not want to talk to them (personal communication, November 10, 2005).

Some musicians and dancers indicated that the behavior of *ludruk* performers who were *waria* went beyond propriety and that *waria* could not control their emotions or sexual desires. In a conversation with some dancers and a drummer, they said that having a *waria* as a girlfriend was dangerous because a *waria*'s character is "hard", their emotions are "strong", and that when they fall in love, it is difficult for them to let go of the person they love. They generalized that *waria* become jealous easily. One man said that he did not want to perform the dance *Ngremo Putri* (*Ngremo* in the female style) when he was in *ludruk* because of *waria*; he did not want to be around them (implying backstage and onstage) so he just performed *Ngremo Lanang* (*Ngremo* in the male style). A drummer agreed, saying that *waria* were also what made him reluctant to play for *ludruk* (personal communication, March 3, 2006). In a different conversation another drummer said that nowadays it is as if *ludruk* performers playing female roles were possessed by mischievous spirits; it was not *ludruk*, but *waria* looking for men (personal communication, June 7, 2006). Many older performers insisted that before the 1990s male *ludruk* performers specializing in female roles did not dress and live as women offstage (although other evidence presented earlier suggests otherwise), linking the presence of *waria* to the disintegration of *ludruk*. Several older performers pointed to the irony that most *ludruk* performers specializing in female roles at the time of my fieldwork could not perform female-style dance well, even though they dressed and lived as women (Sunardi, 2009, pp. 483–484; 2015, pp. 86–87).

Speaking about her own concerns about how *ludruk* performers at the time of my fieldwork were presenting themselves onstage, Mama Samsu further spoke to a sense of responsibility she believed *ludruk* performers specializing in female roles and *waria* must take to present positive images of themselves on- and off-stage so that they would be perceived better in society. She did not care for the fashion show that was part of the opening acts of some *ludruk* performances, finding that it was not polite (*sopan*); the short skirts and tight clothing (often internationally inspired) that performers often modeled, she opined, were inappropriate. As *ludruk* performers and *waria*, she believed that they should be smooth, graceful, and well mannered (*luwes*) and so should wear a long batik cloth, traditional Javanese blouse, and large hair bun (personal communication, May 9 and 16, 2006; Figure 8). This is a "classic" and "traditional" Javanese woman's outfit and hairstyle, although subject to changing trends, too. Mama Samsu was speaking to an expectation of feminine refinement consistent

Figure 8. *Ludruk* performers dance in a traditional outfit for Javanese women. Photograph taken by the author, 2009.

with the dominant Indonesian gender ideologies with which she had grown up even as she insisted that males or individuals assigned male at birth could also embody this ideal of femininity and womanhood.

Identifying offstage behavior that she did not like among younger *waria* active in *ludruk*, Mama Samsu noted that many do not "know themselves" and that they are not faithful to their partners, which can cause problems of jealousy within the *ludruk* community, and even within one group. She did not like the carefree lifestyle she said that many *waria* lead, saying that most do not think about the future and how they will earn a living after their beauty fades. Samsu's concerns about the behavior and future of other *waria* were not unlike the concerns that Tom Boellstorff encountered among gay male and lesbian Indonesians who, feeling a sense of responsibility for bettering the image that larger society had of them, "would castigate each other for only caring about throwing parties, or stealing each other's girlfriends or boyfriends, or gossiping, rather than doing something 'positive' (*positip*)" (2005b, p. 212). Mama Samsu also felt that *waria* needed to take responsibility for themselves and perceptions that others had of them as a strategy for their own betterment and as a strategy for the acceptance of male femininity in daily life (Sunardi, 2015, p. 91). I have come to understand Mama Samsu's attitudes and activism through the lens of respectability politics as she spoke to ways of being—or ways one should be—a respectable *waria* who exudes femininity modeled on dominant constructions of respectable Javanese and Indonesian womanhood.

Observations from the field

Despite the pressures and expectations that Djupri, Muliono, and Mama Samsu identified for males to live as men, and social expectations for male femininities to be restricted to performance, my observations during my fieldwork spanning 2005 to 2007 and subsequent visits indicated a continuity of social needs for male femininity on- and offstage—both in terms of males with women's hearts needing an outlet in which to express and embody their gender identity, and in terms of desires for male femininity on the parts of audiences. Similar to Djupri's experiences in the mid-twentieth century of viewers taking more license with him when they knew he was a male performing female-style dance than with female performers, in the comic routines that preceded *ludruk* performances that I observed, the comedians tended to be freer with their joking, which was often sexual, with males and *waria* performing female roles than with women performing female roles—even kissing males or *waria* playing female roles to the delight of the audience. The *ludruk* performers in female dress played along, feigning anger—anger that a woman would be expected to display if such liberties were taken with her.

These comic scenes were so funny to audiences in part because taking such liberties with women was neither humorous nor tolerated. If guests or audience members danced too closely or attempted to kiss women singer-dancers during *tayub* dance events, for example, the women became angered. They and the men in the group took measures to discourage this behavior from continuing. The women would move away from the man who was breaching the limits of acceptable behavior, either continuing to perform or stopping briefly, looking at the other singers or musicians with visible expressions of exasperation. In extreme cases, men who were ready as bodyguards of sorts would physically remove men behaving this way from the performing space (Sunardi, 2015, pp. 41, 82).

Indicating the ongoing sexual impact of male femininity in 2006, echoing observations from the mid-twentieth century discussed earlier in this chapter, a male musician said that when he sees a man perform female-style dance, such as *Ngremo Putri*, he is affected by the femininity of the dance and the dancer, not the maleness of their biological sex. When he sees men or *waria* performing female roles in *ludruk*, he finds them beautiful, not handsome, noting that they can be more beautiful than women. Admitting that his desire or lust (*nafsu*) cannot always be controlled, he confessed that he has fallen in love with *ludruk* performers who perform female roles, even though he knows they are men. He clarified that he fell in love "just in his heart", meaning that he did not try to pursue a relationship. Asserting his assumptions about the normativity of heterosexuality and yet recognizing the sexual appeal of men or *waria* specializing in female roles, he said that falling in love with a male should not be allowed, but that his feelings were pushed from *nafsu*. He told me that he has many friends who are crazy about *ludruk* performers who specialize in female roles because they have large breasts and are incredibly sexy, even though they are male (personal communication, July 31, 2006; Sunardi, 2009, pp. 476–478; 2015, pp. 85–86; 2022, p. 290).

Other individuals in audiences took pleasure in the beauty of the male and/or *waria* performers who performed female roles. At one *ludruk* performance, a couple of women dancers and I talked about how pretty and feminine one performer was. One woman, who knew I was studying female-style dance, joked that this performer was more beautiful and coquettish than me (personal communication, January 1, 2006). At performances I attended, when the performers dressed as women entered the stage one by one for the *bedayan* chorus portion of the variety acts that preceded the play, men in the audience and running the sound system often whistled for the sexier ones, calling out remarks such as "beautiful!" (*ayu*) and "let's go, beautiful!" (*ayo ayu*). When the performers began to sing, men continued to hoot, whistle, and make comments such as "that which is beautiful!" (*sing ayu*). I observed men act similarly for women singers at performances of *campur sari* (a form of popular music that combines gamelan, keyboard, guitars, drum set, and sometimes other instruments [Brinner, 2008, p. 19; Supanggah, 2003; Cooper, 2015]), indicating that this is one way that men reacted to femaleness regardless of the biological sex of the performer. At one *ludruk* performance, I overheard one man likely in his 50s saying to another man that a particular performer on stage was beautiful, but that one could not really judge from far away—indicating that he was indeed judging. Other people in the audiences of *ludruk* performances acknowledged and delighted in the abilities of the performers to look like beautiful women, saying that they were clever with their makeup.

Like Geertz found in 1950s Java, I encountered a sense of wonder for male and *waria ludruk* performers who specialized in female roles when they were performing. At the *ludruk* shows I attended, audience members' comments indicated that they allowed themselves to be fooled by a good performer or actually were fooled—savoring the confusion. I often overheard men and women of all ages in the audience make comments such as "Is that really a woman?" or "That one looks like a real woman" when performers entered the stage to dance and/or sing. At another performance, a man who was probably in his 40s and I delighted in trying to determine whether one of the performers was really a woman or not. After about 15 minutes, we concluded that the performer was a man. One little girl about six years old sitting next to me at yet another performance was entranced by the female roles, asking me repeatedly if one performer in particular, who happened to be Mama Samsu, was a real woman.

Moreover, as Djupri talked about doing in the 1950s and 1960s, the men and *waria* performers I observed in *ludruk* worked hard to look as feminine as possible. Most wore figure-enhancing undergarments such as corsets. Some wore spandex or spandex-like shorts that gave their buttocks a shapelier, more feminine silhouette. Some males had full breasts, perhaps from hormone therapy or silicone injections (see Boellstorff, 2007, p. 94), indicating that they had more permanently altered the appearance of their bodies. Most spent a considerable amount of time expertly doing their makeup, and some were known to exercise to maintain their figures (personal communication, Luluk Ratna Herawati, January 4, 2006). In cultivating their soprano registers and singing in falsetto, performers took care to sound as female as possible, too. I cannot help but see parallels between what I observed and what Djupri and Mama Samsu shared about their own lives and experiences as artists (Sunardi, 2015, pp. 79–81).

Chapter summary

In exploring Djupri's, Muliono's, and Mama Samsu's lived experiences as artists, I have presented different ways individuals produced male femininity, related to male femininity in on- and offstage contexts, and navigated social pressures within their communities since the mid-twentieth century and into the twenty-first. While Djupri delighted in convincing others that he was a female on- and offstage, he insisted on his manliness in his daily life and distanced himself from a *waria* identity. Muliono performed female-style dance when he was younger as well, but stuck to male-style dances as he came into his own as a young man, future husband, father, and household head. Both Djupri and Muliono spoke to spiritual means that gave them the ability to temporarily embody and exude femaleness, thereby emphasizing that the femaleness was contingent upon the context of performance even as they spoke to their gender fluidity. Mama Samsu lived as a *waria* and used both performance and her offstage life and career to advocate for *waria*'s social acceptance and to model what she believed was respectable behavior and a respectable lifestyle, confidently and boldly embodying and producing male femininity on- and offstage.

While Djupri, Muliono, and Mama Samsu challenged what types of bodies could produce and embody femaleness and thereby challenged dominant Indonesian gender ideologies, they also reinforced dominant ideologies about ideal female subjects through their onstage performances of traditional female-style dance. As Djupri, Muliono, and Mama Samsu negotiated gender representation and identity in Malang on- and offstage, reinforcing gender pluralism and producing male femininity, they contributed to the production of place-based identities as Malangan people. Malangan identities also included articulations of female masculinity as women dancers performed male-style dance, produced complex senses of gender on- and offstage, and negotiated dominant gender norms, topics I explore in the next chapter.

Questions for discussion

1. How did Djupri, Muliono, and Mama Samsu undermine dominant ideologies of gender and sexuality on- and offstage? How did they reinforce dominant ideologies of gender and sexuality?

2. How did Djupri, Muliono, and Mama Samsu navigate pressures from their communities to conform to dominant ideologies of gender and sexuality? (In answering this question, you may wish to also identify what the pressures from their communities were.)

3. How did Djupri, Muliono, and Mama Samsu contribute to the production of local east Javanese identities through their lives and careers as artists? In other words, how did they contribute to what east Javanese, and more specifically, Malangan identities, include?

3
Female masculinity, "layering", and womanhood

As I set out to conduct fieldwork, I did not anticipate that a ghost would be one of the most influential artists I would encounter. I did not imagine that women would be at the center of the creation and adaptation of male-style dances, or that female beauty and sexuality would emanate from male veneers. While in retrospect I see that many of my assumptions about what I might find in Malang reveal more about my own ignorance than anything else, the excitement and wonder I experienced as I encountered more and more about the histories of cross-gender performance pushed me to keep learning, keep listening.

This chapter centers the lives and careers of three women dancers, Muskayah (deceased at the time of my fieldwork), Tri Wahyuningtyas, and Sri Handayani, who produced complex senses of gender through the performance of male-style dance, both challenging and reinforcing dominant constructions of masculinity and femininity through their gender fluidity as they contributed to place-based senses of identity and gender pluralism through the course of the twentieth century (perhaps as early as the late 1890s) and into the twenty-first. Building from my earlier work (Sunardi, 2009, pp. 468–469, 478–480, 485–488; 2013, pp. 148–151; 2015, pp. 33–62, 96–126; 2022, pp. 291–294), I show that in performing male-style dance Muskayah, Tri, and Sri have produced, represented, embodied, and disseminated senses of female masculinity—distinct senses of masculinity produced by females, a concept introduced in Chapter 1 (Halberstam, 1998, pp. 1–2, 15; Blackwood and Wieringa, 2007, pp. 9, 14–15; Blackwood, 2010, p. 29; Sunardi, 2013, p. 141; 2015, p. 11; 2022, p. 290).

The particular senses of female masculinity that Muskayah, Tri, and Sri produced entailed keeping their femaleness visible and/or audible. Halberstam has helped me to understand such approaches as forms of "layering", a theatrical strategy in which a performed gendered role is noticeably superimposed—layered—onto an actor's own gendered self (1998, pp. 260–261). One form of layering occurs "[w]hen a drag king performs as a recognizable male persona" and "choose[s] to allow her femaleness to peek through" (ibid., p. 260). As I show, Muskayah, Tri, and Sri "layered" masculinity onto their female bodies when performing the recognizable male personas portrayed through male-style dances, allowing their femaleness to "peek through" a male veneer. This womanliness in the context of a male-style dance supports Halberstam's point that layering—making visible both the performer's femaleness and the role's maleness—"reveals the permeable boundaries between acting and being" as well as "the artificiality of conventional gender roles" (1998, p. 261). In other words, the concepts of female masculinity and layering offer means to explore how Muskayah, Tri Wahyuningtyas, and

Sri Handayani complicated boundaries between their on- and offstage selves and showed how gender roles are performed cultural constructions.

Paralleling the learning objectives of the previous chapter, by the end of this chapter, my hope is that you will be able to identify ways in which Muskayah, Tri Wahyuningtyas, and Sri Handayani:

1. Challenged and reinforced norms of gender and sexuality on- and offstage;

2. Navigated gender and social pressures (including religious pressures) from the communities in which they lived; and

3. Contributed to the production of local east Javanese identities through their lives and careers as artists.

As you read this chapter, take note of similarities and differences in males' embodiments of femaleness discussed in the previous chapter and females' embodiment of maleness discussed below, a matter I return to at the end of this chapter and in the closing words of this book.

Muskayah: Spiritual dimensions and a legacy of female masculinity and creativity

The spirit of Muskayah, grandmother of the master dancer Djupri who you met in Chapter 2, seemed to be ever present. Djupri and other artists frequently talked about her, referring to stories attributing the creation of Malangan dances to her through spiritual experiences (even if there were various opinions about those stories), her abilities to perform male- and female-style dance, her wide-reaching and impactful career, her skill and knowledge as a musician, and her spiritual power. I was particularly taken with the ways she was remembered to have in effect challenged dominant notions of gender, in part by excelling in realms typically dominated by males, such as playing the drum. I recognize that memories of Muskayah tell us about what was on the rememberer's mind at the time of the conversation, as discussed in Chapter 2 (Neuman, 1993, p. 276; Stoler with Strassler, 2002, p. 170; Zurbuchen, 2005, p. 7; Sunardi, 2015, pp. 25–28). I nonetheless value what we can learn about ways a woman of past times was remembered to have lived her life as an artist and contributed to a legacy of female masculinity and female creativity in Malang and Malangan dances.

As I learned from Djupri over the course of many conversations (who himself learned from Muskayah and other elders as much of what he related occurred well before his birth), Muskayah was born in the 1890s, and given the name Sukanthi. At the age of nine, she fell ill, slipping into a dreamlike trance state. While in this state, the spirit of a legendary princess or noblewoman came to her, calling upon her to heal people by becoming a dancer. This spirit instructed Sukanthi to perform *andhong*, a type of itinerant performance introduced in the previous chapter, and gave her *Beskalan* in the female style, *Beskalan Putri*. This dance, the spirit explained to Sukanthi, existed in the past but had been lost when the last of the great courts of east Java fell hundreds of years ago. Sukanthi recovered briefly before falling ill again. During this second bout, she spoke in a man's voice and received the music and movements of *Beskalan* in the male style, *Beskalan Lanang*.

Upon awakening a few days later, Sukanthi had the ability to perform *Beskalan Putri* and *Beskalan Lanang*, their songs, and the accompanying music. She trained a gamelan ensemble and began to perform, changing her name to Muskayah as a reflection of her new identity as a dancer and healer. (Changing or altering one's name to mark a change in status or stage in life is not unusual in Java.) Initially performing as an *andhong*, Muskayah became famous for her beauty, grace, difficult movements, and efficacious spiritual power to heal through performance. She became particularly known for *Beskalan Putri* because she was so beautiful that people thought it would be a shame if she performed male-style dance. She was asked to perform at events, indicating that her status as a dancer increased as she moved from itinerant to invited performer. While *Beskalan Lanang* ultimately declined in popularity—later to be adapted and popularized in Malang in the 2000s, which I discuss below—she spread *Beskalan Putri* throughout Malang and other parts of Java through her many students and her many performances, including performances in sacred or ritual contexts such as exorcisms, vow fulfillment ceremonies, and village purification ceremonies. *Beskalan Putri* has come to be recognized in and beyond Malang as an iconic Malangan dance, making Muskayah's activity as an artist critical to the production and representation of place-based culture, identity, and senses of femininity through dance performance.

As Djupri explained proudly, Muskayah performed at increasingly prestigious venues as she was hired by the subdistrict in which she lived, the regency, and went all the way to Banyuwangi at the eastern tip of Java and to Yogyakarta in central Java. The sultans of Yogyakarta hired her for her spiritual knowledge, including her abilities to exorcise and make offerings. The Dutch hired her, too, and she performed abroad in the Netherlands, China, and Japan. In addition to performing *Beskalan Putri* and *Beskalan Lanang*, she performed *Ngremo Lanang*, *Ngremo* in the male style. From Djupri's narratives, it seems that Muskayah healed, entertained, and taught many during her long career as an artist, the height of which likely spanned from sometime between 1899 and 1908 to the 1940s, before she passed away in the late 1980s or mid-1990s (Sunardi, 2015, pp. 96–97).

Reinforcement and subversion of gender norms

Although Muskayah seems to have been most well known for her performances of *Beskalan Putri*, I focus on narratives of her embodiments of masculinity to explore how she was remembered to have produced female masculinity. For one, Djupri's narrative about *Beskalan Lanang*'s origins points to uses of spiritual beliefs and practices as a means of challenging dominant constructions of gender at the time I consulted him in 2005–2006. In telling the narrative of *Beskalan Lanang*'s origins, Djupri connected the senses of female masculinity that Muskayah came to embody as a performer of male-style dance to a spiritual experience she had as a child. The image of a little girl speaking in a man's voice suggests a remarkable and powerful manifestation and production of female masculinity (Sunardi, 2015, p. 118).

Muskayah reinforced and subverted gender norms through her performances of male-style dance, or at least gender norms that had become normalized to those remembering her such as Djupri at the time he talked to me. Given that the height of her career likely preceded Indonesian independence (1945), notions of womanhood and social roles women could assume may have been quite different. Responding to my question of whether Muskayah could dance *Ngremo Lanang* like a man, Djupri confirmed,

> Yes. Yes, like a man—it was just her voice. Her voice was a woman's voice, but she imitated a man precisely. It was just that the tones were female tones, but the melody was like a man's.
>
> *Iya. Ya, seperti laki-laki. Hanya suaranya. Suara wanita, tapi meniru orang pria, ya, précis. Hanya nadanya itu, nadanya wanita, tapi lagunya ya, seperti orang laki-laki.* (personal communication, Djupri, January 6, 2006)

In identifying the "male" melodies she sang with her female voice in the course of performing *Ngremo Lanang*, Djupri spoke to how through the use of her voice Muskayah maintained her female-ness and identity as a woman even as she embodied maleness. While reinforcing constructions of masculinity in some ways— such as dancing a male-style dance like a man and singing melodies associated with maleness—she also subverted dominant gender ideologies that separated maleness and femaleness and mapped these constructs to male and female bodies in a one-to-one relationship. She in effect layered maleness over her female body, allowing some of her femaleness to "peek through" as she embodied and produced female masculinity (Halberstam, 1998, p. 260; Sunardi, 2009, pp. 468–469; 2015, pp. 44, 52).

Participation in "male" activities

Although she lived as a woman, marrying and becoming a mother and later a grandmother, by Djupri's accounts Muskayah's embodiment of maleness through dance performance was evident in other realms of her life as she participated in activities typically associated with men in Java, including martial arts, drumming, and spiritual teaching. Expressing his admiration and wonder, Djupri praised her looking strong in a manly way (*gagah*) when she did a form of martial arts called *pencak silat*, recalling:

> Even though Mak Mus was a woman, when she did *pencak silat* she was like this [holds a thumb up]. She was thin, but yes, like this [holds up a thumb]. She looked strong. How could that be?
>
> *Mak Mus dulu itu meskipun wanita, kalau pencak silat, ya gini. Orangnya kecil tugu tapi ya gini. Ya ketoké itu gagah. Kok bisa?* (personal communication, January 6, 2006)

He also remembered her drumming being like a man's and her own goal to be like a man:

> Her drum strokes were distinct, pleasant to listen to—like a man's. "Oh, I have to be like a man", [she said]. She had to be like a man, using whatever way worked. Indeed, when she played "*tak*" it was like a man, just the same. That was the strange thing, but there was indeed, as it may be called, a sacred aspect, *ilmu*.
>
> *Ngendhang ya teges, ya enak, kalau ngendhang. Ya, seperti orang laki. "O aku kudu kaya wong lanang". Harus seperti orang laki-laki, ya opo carané. Ya memang kalau ngetaké ya seperti orang laki-laki. Sama aja. Itu anehnya, tapi memang ada, kalau boleh dikatakan sakral, ilmu.* (personal communication, Djupri, January 6, 2006)

Tak is the name of a drum stroke that is usually quite loud and sharp. Speaking from my own experiences learning to play the drum, it demands a particular strength in the form of a focused energy to execute. By attributing her abilities and physical strength as a drummer and as a dancer to her *ilmu*, Djupri underlined the possession of spiritual knowledge as a strategy of gender transgression in different realms of activity, a strategy we encountered for male performers, including Djupri, embodying femaleness in the previous chapter.

Muskayah also assumed a "male" role as spiritual teacher. While women have been recognized for their spiritual potency and potential, and sometimes have achieved high positions in mystic sects (Geertz, 1960, pp. 328–329; Beatty, 1999, p. 202), the role of teacher or master is typically gendered male as a father figure, and men have usually taken leading roles (Geertz, 1960, p. 329; Beatty, 1999, p. 202; Mulder, 2005, p. 55). In talking about Muskayah as a master of spiritual knowledge as well as her abilities in martial arts and drumming, Djupri remembered and portrayed her as one who pushed at dominant ideas about what women's activities and behaviors should entail. He praised Muskayah, a woman he idolized, not in post-Indonesian independence state-sanctioned terms as a submissive wife and mother, but on her own terms as a dancer, drummer, martial arts expert, spiritually potent person, and spiritual teacher, thereby also subverting post-Indonesian independence ideology about womanhood with which he had grown up. I find the discrepancies between official ideas and social realities, and between official ideas and valued memories of a revered family member, to be striking, showing that the act of remembering can be a form of cultural work and resistance (Sunardi, 2009, pp. 468–469; 2015, p. 58). Indeed, I saw a legacy of female masculinity very much alive in living dancers I came to know directly, including Tri Wahyuningtyas and Sri Handayani.

Tri Wahyuningtyas: Producing Malangness, disseminating female masculinity

Tri Wahyuningtyas (b. 1973) started to dance when she was four years old. She fondly recalled performing for a competition when she was in kindergarten and wanting to know right away how she placed. Although her mother was a dancer and ran her own arts studio, Tri preferred to learn from other people, including her uncle M. Soleh Adi Pramono (b. 1951), a dancer, puppeteer, masked dance narrator, musician, and arts organization director, with whom she often studied. When Tri was in elementary, junior high, and high school, she developed other interests and approached dance more as a hobby than as a serious career path, participating when she felt like it or was asked. After she graduated from high school in 1991, however, she taught dance in junior high and high schools for a couple of years, and M. Soleh Adi Pramono, who believed in her gift for dance, encouraged her to pursue a college degree in the arts. She did so, focusing on dance education. After earning her undergraduate degree in 1997, she taught dance in junior high and high schools, started a master's program, started a family, and in 2004, started teaching dance education at Universitas Negeri Malang (State University of Malang) (personal communication, Tri Wahyuningtyas, July 1, 2006).

While highly skilled in both female and male styles of dance, and an experienced choreographer, Tri explained her specialization in and preference for male-style dance for its strength and for the greater freedom and flexibility permitted by the movement and costume:

> My specialization, I prefer male movement. So that which is strong [in a manly way], rather than perform-ing dance that is for women, girls. As for [names some female-style dances including *Beskalan Putri*], I like them, but just in the sense of "yeah, okay, I can dance them". However, in the sense of total understanding, right, the totality of what I want is to appear strong [in a manly way], to appear with … I am actually more inclined to male style—that which is looser, more pleasant, and the flexibility of the clothing [i.e., costume] that is also male.
>
> *Saya itu spesializasi, lebih suka pada gerakan putra. Jadi yang gagah gitu, daripadi saya menari tari untuk yang perempuan, nanti cewek gitu—seakan Tari Gambyong, [?], Beskalan, itu suka, tetapi dalam pengertian hanya sebatas y's [ya wis] bisa menarinya, tetapi dalam pengertian secara totalitas ya, totalitas ingin apa, yang tampil gagah, tampil dengan ke … itu malah lebih condong ke gaya putra gitu lho, yang lebih los gitu, ya, lebih los, lebih enak gitu, dan flexibilitas apa, pakaian itu juga putra gitu lho.* (personal communication, July 1, 2006)

Tri lived as a woman, but attributed her affinity for male-style dance to her strong personality, further noting that she pre-ferred male-style dance (such as *Beskalan Lanang* and *Ngremo Lanang*) to female-style dance because of its strength and freer movements, reinforcing her point above about its less restrictive clothing (see Figure 4 in Chapter 1):

> Perhaps it is the character, too, the character from the movement that is stronger, also wider and more open. I just feel more comfortable performing it … When I think of female [movement], it is smaller, more, I don't know, one has to—ah, too much! I think it's more intricate than male movement, which is freer and has strength.

> *Mungkin karakter juga, ya, karakter dari gerak itu yang lebih keras, kemudian lebih lebar dan lebih terbuka begitu, saya lebih enak membawakannya itu lho … Kalau saya mikirnya putri, itu lebih kecil, lebih anuh harus—aduh, wis! Saya pikir lebih rumit gitu lho, daripada gerak putra yang lebih bebas dan punya kekuatan gitu lho.* (personal communication, Tri Wahyuningtyas, July 1, 2006)

For Tri, the stage was a space to move and act in ways that felt true to her own self, including ways that were associated with maleness. I believe, too, that the stage was a space wherein she could rehearse and formulate ways of moving and acting that she could take to varying extents into her daily life—that is, being freer in her physical movements and taking on roles of strength and leadership. As a lecturer in the Dance and Music Education Program in the Art and Design Department at State University of Malang, a position she continues to hold at the time of this writing, Tri certainly has been an active career woman and in a position of leadership in the arts community.

In addition to teaching and performing, Tri has expressed her gift for dance through choreography. For example, in 1998, she choreographed *Cucak Ijo*, named for the bird it portrays.

Tri created this dance on the request of the regency of Malang to make a dance that represents its mascot, the *cucak ijo* bird, for its anniversary. In the process of choreographing *Cucak Ijo*, Tri consulted with M. Soleh Adi Pramono who gave her some suggestions, the musician Kusnadi who created the accompanying gamelan music, and the dancer Buari who designed the costumes. Believing it important to document that the dance is her creation she had it copyrighted.

Choreographing *Cucak Ijo* demonstrates not only her creativity as an artist, but her work creating a Malangan dance to celebrate the place of Malang and one of the animals that represents it. In other words, she has contributed to the construction of place-based identity. And in having her dance copyrighted, she recognized, claimed, and documented ownership of her intellectual property, asserting herself as a creative agent. The accompanying music for *Cucak Ijo* is featured on the commercial cassette *Aneka Gending Tari Malangan, Volume 2* (*A Variety of Malangan Dance Compositions, Volume 2*). That Tri is listed as the choreographer for *Cucak Ijo* on this cassette further cements her as its creator and her roles as a creator of Malangan performing arts and artistic leader.

Revival and adaptation of *Beskalan Lanang*

Tri and other women dancers played important roles in the revival and adaptation of the male-style dance *Beskalan Lanang*—a project led by M. Soleh Adi Pramono—making the articulation and production of female masculinity critical in this creative process. As Tri, Soleh, and other artists explained, Soleh initially adapted *Beskalan Lanang* for a folk-dance festival and competition held in Malang in about 2000. During the adaptation process for this festival, Soleh needed a group of five dancers. Since not enough male dancers were active at Soleh's art center, Padepokan Seni Mangun Dharma (PSMD), he selected females, one of whom was Tri (personal communication, Tri Wahyuningtyas, July 3, 2006; M. Soleh Adi Pramono, July 27, 2006).

Believing that Muskayah created *Beskalan Lanang* and that Djupri was heir to her creation after her passing, Soleh brought Djupri to PSMD to teach the dance and its music to the dancers and musicians there; Soleh adapted it by shortening it, adjusting the movements, incorporating influences from other Malangan dances, and developing a floor plan for a group dance (personal communication, Warananingtyas Palupi, November 15, 2005; Djupri, 2006; Tri Wahyuningtyas, July 3, 2006; Kusnadi, July 24, 2006; M. Soleh Adi Pramono, July 27, 2006; Witanto, July 30, 2006; Mujiati, 2004, p. 73). While I have provided more details about how the dance was adapted elsewhere (Sunardi, 2015, pp. 121–125), here I emphasize that it initially was women's bodies, including Tri's, that were vessels and agents for the revival of this Malangan dance and the representation of maleness therein. Given that it was a woman who Djupri and Soleh credited with *Beskalan Lanang*'s creation, I find female masculinity central to its history.

From my own experiences studying and observing this dance, I came to learn that *Beskalan Lanang* is a lively male-style dance portraying a strong male character with a wide leg stance and large arm movements (Figure 4 in Chapter 1). Djupri explained that the dance portrays a man from hundreds of years ago named Djaka Umbaran who has been separated from his true love, Prabaretna (the young woman or girl portrayed in *Beskalan*

Putri), by their parents who forbade their romance. A strong, agile fighter, and a friendly, outgoing youth, the undeterred Djaka Umbaran spends years searching for Prabaretna through the forests with his bow and arrow. Incidentally, *Beskalan Putri* portrays Prabaretna's search for Djaka Umbaran (personal communication, Djupri, February 7, 2006; August 7, 2006; Sunardi, 2015, pp. 98–99). Representations of male handsomeness, physical strength, agility, martial skills, and confidence in *Beskalan Lanang* reinforce dominant Indonesian constructions of masculinity.

Strikingly, given that women have played such important roles in the production and dissemination of *Beskalan Lanang*, sometimes the articulation of masculinity has been inflected with a femaleness that female performers such as Tri have brought to the dance. For example, Tri talked about her conscious decision to do her makeup for male-style dance in a feminine way, generally speaking. During a video session I sponsored to document her performing *Beskalan Lanang*, she explained that she does her makeup "beautifully" for male-style dance. When I asked her why she did this, she said that she did not know; it was normal for her to do so (personal communication, Tri Wahyuningtyas, July 10, 2006). The "beautiful" approach she took for that recording session is evident in Figure 9 in the lines of the eye shadow and liner as well as the "feminine" style of blush. This "beautiful" approach along with the carefully drawn mustache, facial hair below the lower lip, masculine eyebrows, and sideburns makes for a striking juxtaposition of masculinity and femininity that allows her femininity to "peek through" a male veneer, another example of layering that can be an aspect of female masculinity (Halberstam, 1998, pp. 260–261; Sunardi, 2009, pp. 486, 488; 2015, p. 46).

Figure 9. Tri Wahyuningtyas in costume for *Beskalan Lanang*.
Photograph taken by the author, 2006.

Mass dissemination of *Beskalan Lanang*

Around 2002, *Beskalan Lanang* began to be taught in the elementary and junior high schools as part of government-sponsored dance education programs (personal communication, Karen Elizabeth Sekararum, January 6, 2006; Tri Wahyuningtyas, July 3, 2006; Sunardi, 2015, p. 124). Tri played a key role in the dissemination of this dance as one of the dancers who trained elementary and junior high school teachers, who would then teach the dance to the children in the schools of Malang (personal communication, Tri Wahyuningtyas, July 3, 2006; M. Soleh Adi Pramono, July 27, 2006; Witanto, July 30, 2006). Tri reported that the dance was again simplified for mass dissemination to make it easier to teach and learn (personal communication, July 3, 2006). She thus played a key role in the proliferation of *Beskalan Lanang* through her embodiment of female masculinity; when teaching women dancers who would go on to teach girls, she was in effect disseminating female masculinity. For male teachers who would teach girls, female masculinity was also spread as the girls embodied and produced masculinity. I wonder to what extent boys learning the dance from women teachers also learned to embody a certain femininity in their approach—a question for future research.

One of the results of these education efforts was a performance in 2004 by over 1,000 children as a welcoming dance to formally open a stadium in southern Malang, an event attended by the Indonesian President Megawati Sukarnoputri (personal communication, M. Soleh Adi Pramono, July 27, 2006; Witanto, July 30, 2006). It is noteworthy that a male-style dance so influenced by females and female masculinity was performed at an opening ceremony attended by the first female president of Indonesia, another woman taking on a role largely gendered as male.

As an aid for dance teachers in the schools, Soleh included *Beskalan Lanang* on a VCD of Malangan dances released by PSMD in 2003, *Tari Tradisional Malangan* (*Traditional Malangan Dance*). Notably, all male dancers were used for the video, including dancers Soleh recruited and trained for the project (personal communication, Witanto, July 30, 2006). By making such a concerted effort to recruit men to dance for the video, a more permanent artifact and reference material—whereas he did not do so for the festival performance, a more ephemeral presentation of the dance—Soleh revealed his preference for the dance as a male-style dance performed by men and his belief that it should be represented as such, rather than as a cross-gender dance inflected with female masculinity. He in effect reinforced dominant Indonesian notions of gender that map masculinity to men's bodies for the video, contributing to productions and representations of male masculinity (Sunardi, 2015, p. 124).

At the time of my fieldwork spanning 2005–2007, although both men and women performed *Beskalan Lanang* (and to my knowledge still do), when the dance was performed by a group of teenagers and/or adults, it seemed to most often be performed by groups of the same gender. Tri explained that when she performed in a group, it was always with other women. She said that she had heard about a performance that was mixed, but she did not participate in it. She explained that women and men dancing the same dance as a group would not look balanced on stage in terms of their body height and strength of movement

(personal communication, July 3, 2006). I have come to understand the differences that Tri identified as differences between
articulations of male masculinity and female masculinity, reinforcing Halberstam's point that female and male masculinity are distinct (1998). The dancer B. Supriono Hadi Prasetya explained that
when he performed the dance in a group, he always performed
with other men. He did not recall seeing a mixed gender performance, although he had heard about the 2004 mass performance by children, which involved both boys and girls (personal
communication, June 27, 2006). This suggests a certain flexibility or allowance for children, who have not yet gone through
puberty, to represent masculinity together as a mixed group.

Internalization of maleness

In performing male-style dance, Tri internalized the maleness
of the characters she portrayed, contributing to the production
of female masculinity, and, I suggest, a form of internal gender
crossing. She embodied maleness by concentrating from the
heart. She talked about the importance of becoming the character from the dancer's heart or soul, explaining that if there were
no disturbances, she felt like the male character she was portraying and no longer herself. As a dancer, she expounded, one
must be able to feel the character and have enthusiasm from
the inside, otherwise the dance will not have form. In speaking
about feeling like the male character in the context of performance, Tri was also speaking about the contingency of taking on
masculinity (Sunardi, 2009, p. 488; 2015, pp. 59–60).

As I have argued elsewhere, in making her womanliness obvious in her articulation of female masculinity, Tri was making it

obvious that she was a woman even as she performed male-style dance. This, I suggest, was to show that as a woman she could be like a man—she could demonstrate physical strength, she could move freely, she could be a creative agent and she could and did take leading roles in the arts community of which she was part (Sunardi, 2015, pp. 61–62). The projection of femininity through a male-style dance was all the more obvious in the dance *Ngremo Tayub*, as exemplified by Sri Handayani, to whom I turn next.

Sri Handayani: Female masculinity in *Ngremo Tayub*

When I interviewed Sri Handayani (b. 1982) in 2006 she was quite in demand as a singer and dancer, frequently performing for *tayub* dance events and frequently performing the dance *Ngremo Tayub*. She came from a family of artists and as a young girl started to study dance with her mother. She recalled going with her mother to performances, seeing her mother perform *Ngremo*, and practicing at home. By the time Sri was in junior high, she was performing as well, but with her mother, following her mother's lead as Sri did not yet feel ready to perform on her own. Her mother would dance behind the stage and cue Sri. Or, for shadow puppet theater performances in which Sri sang, her mother would sing in her ear and Sri would sing out loud. Sri felt ready to perform as an independent artist toward the end of junior high, and she ended up leaving school because she became so busy as a performer. She performed mostly for *tayub* dance events, but also for shadow puppet theater and the popular music form *campur sari* (personal communication, Sri Handayani, March 29, 2006). I found Sri a beautiful singer and dancer, and was most taken with her activity performing the male-style dance *Ngremo Tayub*.

Creativity of women dancers

Ngremo Tayub's history is strongly connected to the creativity of women dancers and the articulation of female masculinity (Sunardi, 2009, p. 485; 2015, pp. 54–55). *Ngremo Tayub* is a variation of the iconic east Javanese dance *Ngremo Lanang* (*Ngremo* in the male style) that women dancers created in the context of *tayub* dance events. These events, also called *tayuban*, feature professional female entertainers who are hired to sing and dance for a host's guests and are accompanied by a gamelan ensemble (Hefner, 1987; Hughes-Freeland, 1993; Widodo, 1995). Performers recalled that by the late 1970s to mid-1980s, a section in which viewers could tip the performers, request a song, and dance with the dancers was incorporated into *Ngremo Lanang*, which female singer-dancers performed as an opening dance (personal communication, Kusnadi, November 17, 2005; Anik Nurdjanah, February 9, 2006, February 21, 2006; Achmad Suwarno, April 3, 2006; Asbari, June 29, 2006; Sri Utami, August 3, 2006; Ngatmuji, August 12, 2006). By the 1990s, a distinct substyle that came to be called *Ngremo Tayub* had emerged. Although this style was named for *tayub*, it is performed for a variety of types of performances, not just for *tayub*, and may be performed with or without a tipping section. Some performers called *Ngremo* performed with a tipping section *Ngremo Tembel* or *Ngremo Tembelan*. Some referred to *Ngremo Tayub* as *Ngremo Tembel* as well.

Ngremo Tayub offers one of the most obvious examples of the ways women layered maleness onto their femaleness to produce female masculinity, which I focus on in this and the next three sections (Sunardi, 2009, pp. 485–486; 2013, pp. 149–151; 2015, pp. 43–55; 2022, pp. 291–294). I learned from Sri and other performers that movements associated with masculinity—higher arm positions, wider leg stances, and larger head movements—included those drawn from various male-style dances and from *pencak silat* martial arts (personal communication, Karen Elizabeth Sekararum, November 29, 2005, January 6, 2006; Madya, December 17, 2005; Cuci Indrawati, December 21, 2005; Sri Handayani, March 29, 2006; Sri Utami, August 3, 2006; Kusnadi, 2005–2006). Females, however, tended to articulate these movements in a more supple manner than males did for male-style dances and martial arts, allowing a certain grace and fluidity that are associated with female-style dances (and femaleness more broadly) to permeate the execution of their movements. Other movements were associated more directly with femaleness, such as movements drawn from aerobics—typically a woman's activity—and from "pat-a-cake" hand games—movements associated with children's activities. Movements associated with femaleness juxtaposed with those associated with maleness but executed in a more supple manner in the context of a male-style dance performed by female bodies contributed to the production of a complex sense of gender.

The feminization of the movements of male-style dance in *Ngremo Tayub* was not always valued, however, as evident in some performers' critiques of *Ngremo Tayub* for looking too feminine. One dancer and vocalist, a woman born in the 1950s, criticized *Ngremo Tayub* dancers "nowadays" (at the time I consulted her in 2006) for executing a head roll inappropriately for male-style dance. She found that their head movements were not sharp or clearly articulated enough—too supple—for male-style dance, declaring that the movement was from *Ngremo Putri* (*Ngremo* in the female style). Another dancer, a man born in the 1960s, commented that the movements did not fit the knightly character being portrayed and made the dance too coquettish. In critiquing the ways in which female dancers combined masculinity and femininity, these artists in effect expressed their discomfort with the ways dancers were disrupting separations of maleness and femaleness that they had come to accept as normal and fitting for male and female styles of *Ngremo*. Indeed, when women performed other male-style dances, such as *Ngremo Lanang*, *Beskalan Lanang*, and male-style masked dances, they tended to execute the movements more fluidly than male dancers, similarly allowing their femaleness to "peek through" (Halberstam, 1998, pp. 260–261).

When women performed male-style dance, in most cases, but not all, performers and audiences were aware that dancers were female. Paradoxically, this awareness reinforced the separation of maleness and femaleness in dominant Indonesian gender ideologies even as performers like Sri Handayani performed gender fluidity as they produced female masculinity. For the most part, performing male-style dance did not detract from the performers' womanhood because usually the femaleness of the dancer's biological sex had a stronger impact on those watching than the maleness of the dance style—although this could depend on the dance and the dancer. One musician generalized that when he sees women perform male-style dance, the feminine aspects of the dancer and the dance affect him, and he finds the dancer beautiful, not handsome (personal communication, July 31, 2006).

Another musician, born in the mid-1940s, articulated his discomfort with one of the movements that has become characteristic of *Ngremo Tayub*—lifting the fist above the head. He repeatedly explained that according to traditional conventions, lifting the hand above the head was impolite because this movement displayed the armpit. He implied that it was inappropriate for women to display their armpits—which were clearly visible when the arms were lifted high because the costume was sleeveless (Figure 10). His comment indicated that he was seeing the dancers' femaleness first and foremost. He saw that the maleness was layered onto the dancers' female bodies, but he still held the dancers to dominant standards of "polite" womanhood, thereby reinforcing a separation between maleness and femaleness while also speaking to the dancers' femaleness. Despite critiques from some performers, the ways in which females pushed at assumptions about gender—in effect combining maleness and femaleness—made their performances of male-style dance interesting for many viewers. The dancer and vocalist Karen Elizabeth Sekararum interpreted the subversion of gender in *Ngremo Tayub* as part of the dance's appeal (personal communication, November 29, 2005).

Costume and makeup

In addition to the dance movements, the subversion of gender can be understood in the ways Sri Handayani and other dancers highlighted their femininity through the costume and makeup

Figure 10. Sri Handayani (a female) models a costume and makeup for
Ngremo Tayub. Photograph taken by the author, 2006.

for *Ngremo Tayub*. Karen Elizabeth Sekararum explained that the womanhood of the dancer is emphasized through the costume, jewelry, and makeup, despite the mustache that is penciled on and the maleness of the dance style (personal communication, November 29, 2005). The femininity that Karen Elizabeth drew my attention to, and that I observed in performances of *Ngremo Tayub*, can be seen by comparing photographs of Sri modeling a *Ngremo Tayub* costume (Figure 10) and male *Ngremo Lanang* dancers performing in *ludruk* theater (Figure 11).

As seen in Figure 10, Sri Handayani does not look like a biological male, but instead looks like a woman trying to look sort of like a man. Sri's costume, with its strapless top and vest, differs from the males' long-sleeved shirts, and her female figure is enhanced through the cut of the top and the way she has fastened it. Sri's bare arms reinforce her womanliness and are rather erotic in a Muslim context in which many women cover their shoulders and the top part of their arms, if not most or all of their arms, in public. She has on a wig of short hair, and a male-style head cloth. Makeup was another means by which Sri and other *Ngremo Tayub* dancers undermined ideological separations between maleness and femaleness. Sri used cosmetics to make her femaleness apparent. The false eyelashes and the pink and purple colors of the eye makeup are recognizably feminine according to conventions of east Javanese dance makeup. The blush on her cheeks is softer than the blush on the male dancers in Figure 11. Although not clearly visible in this photograph, she has not used a pencil to thicken the fine hairs on the side of her face to create thick, more "manly" sideburns.

Figure 11. Males perform *Ngremo Lanang* for a performance of *ludruk*. Photograph taken by the author, 2006.

While some *Ngremo Tayub* dancers were producing a sense of female masculinity by doing their makeup in a more "feminine" manner, one reason they did so was practical, related to the convention of changing gendered outfits during a performance event. In many cases, after the dancer(s) performed *Ngremo Tayub*, she or they left the stage and changed into feminine attire of a long batik cloth wrapped tightly around the lower body and tightly fitting blouse, often made of lace. They redid their hair, replacing their male-style wig with a large bun, and adjusted their makeup to appear like Sri in Figure 12. Returning to the stage, they performed as female vocalists seated with the gamelan (e.g., for shadow puppet performances) or female singer-dancers (e.g., for *tayub* or *campur sari*). By doing their

Figure 12. Sri Handayani, performing as a singer-dancer for a *tayub* event, wears feminine attire. Photograph taken by the author, 2006.

makeup in a more feminine manner for *Ngremo Tayub*, the danc-ers could more quickly change from their *Ngremo* costume and makeup to female-style dress.

Speaking further to practical considerations and also to eco-nomic ones, Sri explained that changing quickly for *tayub* is necessary; otherwise, the guests will go home and the dancers will not earn as much money (personal communication, March 29, 2006). Sometimes other women who had not performed *Ngremo* were already dressed in female attire and performed while the *Ngremo* dancer(s) changed outfits. Once changed, the *Ngremo* dancers joined these women—although sometimes a dancer was hired just to perform *Ngremo*, as Sri sometimes was (personal communication, March 29, 2006).

The convention of changing gendered outfits was another means by and through which Sri and other *Ngremo Tayub* danc-ers subverted separations of maleness from femaleness, as well as performed contingent senses of gender and gender fluidity. Women embodied different gendered personas during different points in the performance, showing that masculinity and femi-ninity were, in part, the product of makeup and dress—not fixed, inherent aspects of the anatomy—and were contingent upon context (Blackwood, 2010). Through the transformation in the dressing room, the dancers—displaying gender fluidity—were able to reemerge in all of their feminine glory, assuming a hyper-feminine persona characteristic of the stage image cultivated by female singers and dancers in many parts of Java (Spiller, 2007, p. 41).

Furthermore, *Ngremo Tayub* dancers including Sri, as have other cross-dressed performers, played with dominant expectations about gender. Writing about drag kinging in the United States (with some reference to London), Judith Halberstam observes that "mainstream coverage of the scene tends to evince the sincere hope that even though girls will be boys, they will eventually return to being very attractive girls" (1998, p. 261). Likewise, I suggest that viewers in Java imagined the attractive femininity that lay under the "surface" of the *Ngremo Tayub* costume. The contrast of the dancers' appearance in the *Ngremo* costume and in female attire ultimately enhanced the dancers' beauty when they reappeared in female dress, reinforcing both the dancers' womanhood as well as the contingent female masculinity of *Ngremo Tayub*. At the same time, returning to Judith Butler's points presented in Chapter 1 (1990; 1993; 1999), it showed that gender is very much a product of "doing", making more transparent that an individual can fluidly move between "doing" gender or genders in different ways.

Heterosexual, homoerotic, and hyperfeminine representations

Ngremo Tayub dancers' appearance reinforced and undermined dominant norms as dancers interacted with guests (usually male) during the *tembelan* (tipping) section. As mentioned, this section—in which viewers may tip the performers, request a song, and dance with the dancers—may be inserted into *Ngremo Tayub*. The *tembelan* section reinforced heterosexuality and allowed space for homoerotic imaginations. Usually those who requested songs were men. The interaction of these men and the dancers' quasi-male-looking bodies in the performance space displayed a type of male homoeroticism, but one tempered by the knowledge that the dancers were female and, in many cases, would reappear later in the evening in feminine attire. This homoeroticism was permissible because the representation of a heterosexual relationship underlay the interaction. In cases where a woman danced with the *Ngremo Tayub* dancers (which I observed only once), a female homoeroticism was evoked as most—if not everyone—present knew the *Ngremo Tayub* dancers were women, too. Complicating matters, women dancing with female dancers in male-style costumes reinforced representations of heterosexuality. This cultural space for the simultaneous imagination of both homoeroticism and heterosexuality was another way participants in the performance event (including dancers, musicians, hosts, and guests) pushed at dominant social norms that insisted on the normalcy of heterosexuality and made space for gender pluralism and fluidity within the dominant framework of gender dualism (Peletz, 2006).

Ngremo Tayub dancers usually sing in the course of performing, as did Sri. As in other styles of *Ngremo*, dancers typically sing welcoming texts and a form of poetry called *parikan*, among other texts (Sunardi, 2015, pp. 51–54; 2023). As indicated, they also sing requested songs during the *tembelan* section when *tembelan* is included. I suggest that the sound of a recognizably female voice emanating from a female body in the *Ngremo* costume and makeup—with its juxtapositions of maleness and femaleness—further contributed to the pleasure and disruption of this dance. Although the *Ngremo Tayub* dancers did not appear as hyperfeminine figures when in the *Ngremo* costume, their singing reminded viewers that hyperfeminine women lay under the "surface" of masculinity.

Writing about Sundanese dance events in West Java that feature female entertainers, the ethnomusicologist Henry Spiller has argued that the image of the hyperfeminine singer-dancer "brings the imagined oppositions of masculine and feminine, so vital to gender ideology, into sharp relief" (2007, p. 41). In many performances featuring *Ngremo Tayub*, the "imagined oppositions" of maleness and femaleness were brought into "sharp relief", too, albeit in some different ways. These ways included the "feminine-masculine" appearance of *Ngremo Tayub* dancers such as Sri; participants' knowledge that, in many cases, the *Ngremo Tayub* dancer would reappear as a hyperfeminine woman; and the sound of a female voice emanating from the dancer's quasi-male-looking body when the dancers sing.

Women, power, and money

The ways performers talked about *Ngremo Tayub*'s history also has implications related to women's power and their singing. The incorporation of the *tembelan* section, in which guests could request a song, inspired a bit of controversy among performers. Some (who were primarily male) said almost with disgust that this was just a way for the dancers to make more money. They seemed to be implying that this innovation to *Ngremo* was economically driven and had little artistic merit, suggesting that they were interpreting this change through the lens of the dominant, aristocratic, male-oriented Javanese ideology of power that links concerns with money to crudeness (Djajadiningrat-Nieuwenhuis, 1987; Anderson, 1990; Keeler, 1990; Brenner, 1995; 1998; Weiss, 2006, pp. 55–56; Sears, 2007, pp. 54–58; Sunardi, 2015, p. 3; 2022, pp. 290–291). Performers may have also internalized official views that the presence of "desire and cash" is what makes female singer-dancers and their performances "deemed unsuitable as approved national culture" (Hughes-Freeland, 2008c, p. 144). In the eyes of some, inserting a tipping section was inappropriate for the brave, proud, knightly male character of *Ngremo Lanang*, a dance that was usually performed to welcome and honor guests; a tipping section, in the eyes of some performers, effectively degraded the dance into a display of money.

I cannot help but speculate that the ambivalence about the tipping innovation was also connected to women's control of the money. Significantly more tip money went to the female dancers, rather than to the male musicians, and it was largely a dancer's decision as to whether she would share her tips and how much she would share with the musicians (usually with the drummer). In other words, females made an innovation that augmented women's economic power, even though it may not have augmented their status. Similarly, Susan Browne found that the tip money earned by female *dangdut* singers in nightclubs, although providing a means of giving them economic status, "does not enhance their social status" (2000, p. 16). Guests' requests for songs and paying tips did, however, give women a certain economic authority to "rule the roost" as they performed *Ngremo*, as many women have done in the home despite dominant Indonesian ideologies that women should be subservient wives (Brenner, 1995).

Legitimization through religious discourse

Performing male-style dance was also a means by and through which Sri and other women negotiated Islamic orthodoxy and piety (Sunardi, 2013, p. 148; 2015, pp. 60–61). "Because Islam has comprehensive teachings about women's role and place in society", Susan Blackburn instructively writes, "almost anything women do can be seen to be political in the sense of either accepting, supporting or challenging religious practices and beliefs" (2008, p. 84). Sri, who identified as Muslim, responded to my question as to whether she ever felt any incompatibility with her religious beliefs by explaining,

> No, that is our work, you know. Why should we feel ashamed, why? It is our work, right, our work in order to eat, right? As far as religious matters, that is between us and the one above. Yes, so [work and religion] cannot be all mixed up. The important thing is that we are right, yes?—Work a job that is *halal*.
>
> *Nggak, kita kan ya 'is, perkerjaan itu, mbak. Kenapa harus opo ya, malu, kenapa? Kita kan, kerja kan, kerja to, untuk makan? Kalau, kalau urusan agama kita ya sama yang di atas gini. Ya, jadi nggak boleh dicampur aduk. Yang penting kita benar gitu aja, ya? Kerjaé halal gitu.* (personal communication, Sri Handayani, March 29, 2006)

In using the word "*halal*"—what is permitted or allowed by Islam—Sri evoked the religion to legitimize her profession as an artist, in some ways a striking assertion given the immoral, licentious stereotype of female singer-dancers in Java, as well as her activity performing male-style dance. Invoking Islamic discourse, she was insisting on the "rightness" of her profession.

Other Muslim female performers have drawn on religious discourse to legitimize their professions, offering additional examples of "women shaping Islam" (van Doorn-Harder, 2006). Such performers have included other East Javanese female singer-dancers that Robert Hefner encountered who performed in *tayub* dance events, including female singer-dancers from Malang; he found that "[v]irtually all ... claim to be Muslim, some insisting quite strenuously that they are good Muslims" (1987, p. 77). Female *dangdut* singers—including the infamous Inul Daratista who was at the center of national controversy in the early 2000s for a style of dancing that some Indonesians found to be too sexually provocative—have also positioned themselves as Muslims, maintaining that their art and their religion were separate matters (Daniels, 2009, pp. 88–89; 2013, pp. 169–170; Bader, 2011, p. 346). Other *dangdut* singers negotiated Islam and their profession through their belief that the money earned as an entertainer at a place where alcohol was consumed was *halal* as long as they did not drink the alcohol themselves (Browne, 2000, p. 29).

As they negotiated Islam, Sri and other female performers were subverting dominant Indonesian gender ideologies that insisted that women be "proper wives and mothers", making cultural space for women—including Muslim women—to publicly assert other roles (e.g., as artists) as well as their sexuality (Browne, 2000, pp. 2, 30), while also countering negative stereotypes of women performers. Doing so through the performance of male-style dances, as Sri did when she performed *Ngremo Tayub*, made such negotiations of gender and religion all the more complex (Sunardi, 2013).

Chapter summary

In exploring the lives and careers of Muskayah, Tri Wahyuningtas, and Sri Handayani, this chapter has offered sketches of three women who have produced complex senses of gender through the performance of male-style dance over the course of the twentieth century (perhaps since the late 1890s) and into the twenty-first. All three women contributed to the production, representation, and continuity of female masculinity, and senses of female masculinity that entailed keeping their femaleness visible and/or audible, exemplifying Halberstam's concept of "layering" as a theatrical strategy in which a performed gendered role is noticeably superimposed—layered—onto an actor's own gendered self (1998, pp. 260–261). Muskayah, Tri, and Sri have thereby made it more visible that masculinity and femininity are constructions and performed identities—that is, they are "done" rather than inherent to biological sex and that people can move between them, contributing to gender fluidity and pluralism. While Muskayah, Tri, and Sri lived as women in their offstage lives—all three had married men and were mothers—the roles of wife and mother were certainly not the only aspects of their rich identities and lives as artists and as women.

As we saw with Djupri, Muliono, and Mama Samsu in the previous chapter, Muskayah, Tri, and Sri negotiated gender representation and identity in Malang on- and offstage. In doing so, all six dancers reinforced gender pluralism and contributed to the production of place-based identities as Malangan people. Stepping back to further reflect on the ways Djupri, Muliono, Mama Samsu, Muskayah, Tri, and Sri navigated and negotiated dominant gender ideologies through their lived experiences as dancers brings me to the closing words in the next chapter that conclude this book.

Questions for discussion

1. How did Muskayah, Tri Wahyuningtyas, and Sri Handayani challenge and reinforce norms of gender and sexuality on- and offstage?

2. How did Muskayah, Tri Wahyuningtyas, and Sri Handayani navigate gender and social pressures (including religious pressures) from the communities in which they lived?

3. How did Muskayah, Tri Wahyuningtyas, and Sri Handayani contribute to the production of local east Javanese identities through their lives and careers as artists?

4. What similarities and differences do you notice in males' embodiments of femaleness discussed in the previous chapter and in females' embodiment of maleness discussed in this chapter?

4
Closing words

As I often like to say to students upon a course's completion or when making graduation remarks, I hope that you are *not* satisfied. I hope that you have many questions remaining and continue learning, reading, observing, listening, researching, questioning, and thinking. It is my hope that some of the discussion questions and assignment ideas that follow might lead you to new research projects, which might someday become publications that advance scholarly and general understandings of gender.

The six artists I have foregrounded in this book are just a few of the many incredible individuals I was fortunate enough to meet, learn from, watch, hear about, and listen to over the course of my fieldwork in and visits to Malang. This book has focused on ways Djupri, Muliono, Mama Samsu, Muskayah, Tri Wahyuningtyas, and Sri Handayani fashioned femininities and made masculinities, exploring gender as a cultural construction that people continuously produce, reproduce, contest, challenge, alter, and so on— in short, negotiate. Through the analytical frameworks of gender performativity and intersectionality, this book has explored ways we can understand processes by and through which individuals negotiate gender through the performing arts and their lived experiences as artists in specific cultural contexts. In centering the lived experiences and perspectives of six dancers, I have presented some of the ways individuals contributed to the cultural production of gender on- and offstage as they navigated dominant norms in Malang, highlighting themes of onstage–offstage gender negotiations, gender fluidity, gender pluralism, and spirituality. I have argued that the production and representation of gender and place-based identity informed each other as dancers contributed to the production of Malangan styles of performance as distinct substyles within the cultural region of east Java.

Performers produced complex senses of gender, including male femininity, female masculinity, and contingent senses of gender. Something that has interested me is that male femininity and female masculinity are not entirely analogous. In many cases when males took on male femininity, they worked hard to pass as female, while when females took on female masculinity, they kept their womanliness visible. In other publications, which I invite you to explore, I have built from other scholars' work to suggest that there is an underlying femaleness or female power in dances performed as cross-gender dances in Malang that is connected to centuries-old Indic notions (Becker, 1988, pp. 385, 388; 1991, p. 116; 1993, pp. 3, 8, 128; Hughes-Freeland, 1995, p. 198; Sunardi, 2015, p. 3; 2020, p. 454; 2022, p. 291). Indeed, I hope that you are inspired to continue to learn more about Javanese and Indonesian cultures, and the compelling, creative, and courageous ways people in various cultural and historical contexts around the world negotiate, navigate, and produce gender.

Discussion questions and project/ assignment ideas

1. What are three ways dance performance in Malang provides cultural space in which gender norms can be reinforced, subverted, challenged, navigated, and so on—sometimes simultaneously?

2. What are three examples of complex senses of gender that both push at and reinforce a culturally dominant heterosexual, male–female gender binary in Malang?

3. How does the specific cultural context of Malang impact the ways dancers have negotiated gender on- and offstage?

4. Applying theoretical and methodological approaches used in this book, what are some of the ways performance traditions in your community, or in another culture or time period, provide social space in which gender norms can be reinforced, subverted, challenged, navigated, and so on? How does the specific cultural context inform ways in which performers do so on- and offstage?

5. How might you build from the theoretical and methodological approaches used in this book to develop new approaches that are informed by a performing tradition of your choice and its cultural and/or historical context?

References

Anderson, B. R. O'G. (1990). The idea of power in Javanese culture. In: *Language and Power: Exploring Political Cultures in Indonesia*. Ithaca: Cornell University Press, pp. 17–77.

Anderson, B. R. O'G. (1996). "Bullshit!" s/he said: The happy, modern, sexy, Indonesian married woman as transsexual. In: L. J. Sears, ed., *Fantasizing the Feminine in Indonesia*. Durham: Duke University Press, pp. 270–294.

Bader, S. (2011). Dancing Bodies on Stage: Negotiating *Nyawer* Encounters at *Dangdut* and *Tarling Dangdut* Performances in West Java. *Indonesia and the Malay World*, 39(115), pp. 333–355.

Beatty, A. (1999). *Varieties of Javanese Religion: An Anthropological Account*. Cambridge: Cambridge University Press.

Becker, J. (1988). Earth, Fire, *Sakti*, and the Javanese Gamelan. *Ethnomusicology*, 32(3), pp. 385–391.

Becker, J. (1991). The Javanese court Bedhaya dance as a tantric analogy. In: J. C. Kassler, ed., *Metaphor: A Musical Dimension*. Sydney: Currency Press, pp. 109–120.

Becker, J. (1993). *Gamelan Stories: Tantrism, Islam, and Aesthetics in Central Java*. Program for Southeast Asian Studies, Arizona State University.

Blackburn, S. (2008). Indonesian Women and Political Islam. *Journal of Southeast Asian Studies*, 39(1), pp. 83–105.

Blackwood, E. (2005). Gender Transgression in Colonial and Postcolonial Indonesia. *Journal of Asian Studies*, 64(4), pp. 849–879.

Blackwood, E. (2007). Transnational sexualities in one place: Indonesian readings. In: S. E. Wieringa, E. Blackwood, and A.

Bhaiya, eds., *Women's Sexualities and Masculinities in a Globalizing Asia*. New York: Palgrave Macmillan, pp. 181–199.

Blackwood, E. (2010). *Falling Into the Lesbi World: Desire and Difference in Indonesia*. Honolulu: University of Hawai'i Press.

Blackwood, E., and S. E. Wieringa. (2007). Globalization, sexuality, and silences: Women's sexualities and masculinities in an Asian context. In: S. E. Wieringa, E. Blackwood, and A. Bhaiya, eds., *Women's Sexualities and Masculinities in a Globalizing Asia*. New York: Palgrave Macmillan, pp. 1–20.

Boellstorff, T. (2004a). The Emergence of Political Homophobia in Indonesia: Masculinity and National Belonging. *Ethnos*, 69(4), pp. 465–486.

Boellstorff, T. (2004b). Playing Back the Nation: *Waria*, Indonesian Transvestites. *Cultural Anthropology*, 19(2), pp. 159–195.

Boellstorff, T. (2005a). Between Religion and Desire: Being Muslim and *Gay* in Indonesia. *American Anthropologist*, 107(4), pp. 575–585.

Boellstorff, T. (2005b). *The Gay Archipelago: Sexuality and Nation in Indonesia*. Princeton: Princeton University Press.

Boellstorff, T. (2007). *A Coincidence of Desires: Anthropology, Queer Studies, Indonesia*. Durham: Duke University Press.

Brenner, S. A. (1995). Why women rule the roost: Rethinking Javanese ideologies of gender and self-control. In: A. Ong and M. G. Peletz, eds., *Bewitching Women, Pious Men: Gender and Body Politics in Southeast Asia*. Berkeley: University of California Press, pp. 19–50.

Brenner, S. A. (1996). Reconstructing Self and Society: Javanese Muslim Women and "The Veil". *American Ethnologist*, 23(4), pp. 673–697.

Brenner, S. A. (1998). *The Domestication of Desire: Women, Wealth, and Modernity in Java*. Princeton: Princeton University Press.

Brinner, B. (2008). *Music in Central Java: Experiencing Music, Expressing Culture*. New York: Oxford University Press.

Brown, R. L. (2020). *The Heart of a Woman: The Life and Music of Florence B. Price*. Urbana, Chicago, and Springfield: University of Illinois Press.

Browne, S. (2000). The Gender Implications of Dangdut Kampungan: Indonesian "Low-Class" Popular Music. Centre of Southeast Asian Studies Working Paper 109. Clayton, Victoria [Australia]: Monash Asia Institute, Monash University.

Butler, J. (1990). Performative acts and gender constitution: An essay in phenomenology and feminist theory. In: S.-E. Case, ed., *Performing Feminisms: Feminist Critical Theory and Theatre*. Baltimore: The Johns Hopkins University Press, pp. 270–282.

Butler, J. (1993). *Bodies That Matter: On the Discursive Limits of "Sex"*. New York: Routledge.

Butler, J. (1999). *Gender Trouble: Feminism and the Subversion of Identity*. New York: Routledge.

Cho, S., Crenshaw, K. W. and McCall, L. (2013). Toward a Field of Intersectionality Studies: Theory, Applications, and Praxis. *Signs*, 38(4), pp. 785–810.

Cooper, N. I. (2015). Retuning Javanese Identities: The Ironies of a Popular Genre. *Asian Music*, 46(2), pp. 55–88.

Crawford, M. (2001). East Java. In: S. Sadie, ed., *The New Grove Dictionary of Music and Musicians*. Vol. 12. Executive editor John Tyrrell. New York: Grove, pp. 329–335.

Crenshaw, K. (1991). Mapping the Margins: Intersectionality, Identity Politics, and Violence Against Women of Color. *Stanford Law Review*, 43(6), pp. 1241–1299.

Daniels, T. (2009). *Islamic Spectrum in Java*. Burlington, VT: Ashgate Publishing Company.

Daniels, T.P. (2013). Social drama, *dangdut*, and popular culture. In: T. P. Daniels, ed., *Performance, Popular Culture, and Piety in Muslim Southeast Asia*. New York: Palgrave Macmillan, pp. 161–177.

Del Negro, G. P. and Berger, H. M. (2004). Identity reconsidered, the world doubled. In: H. M. Berger and G. P. Del Negro, *Identity and Everyday Life: Essays in the Study of Folklore, Music, and Popular Culture*. Middletown: Wesleyan University Press, pp. 124–157.

Djajadiningrat-Nieuwenhuis, M. (1987). Ibuism and Priyayization: Path to power? In: E. Locher-Scholten and A. Niehof, eds., *Indonesian Women in Focus: Past and Present Notions*. Dordrecht: Foris Publications, pp. 43–51.

Douglas, G. (2010). *Music in Mainland Southeast Asia: Experiencing Music, Expressing Culture*. New York: Oxford University Press.

Foley, K. (1985). The Dancer and the Danced: Trance Dance and Theatrical Performance in West Java. *Asian Theatre Journal*, 2(1), pp. 28–49.

Frederick, W. H. (1982). Rhoma Irama and the Dangdut Style: Aspects of Contemporary Indonesian Popular Culture. *Indonesia*, 34, pp. 102–130.

Geertz, C. (1960). *The Religion of Java*. Chicago: The University of Chicago Press.

Green, J., Denny, D. and Cromwell, J. (2018). "What Do You Want Us to Call You?" Respectful Language. *TSG: Transgender Studies Quarterly*, 5(1), pp. 100–110.

Halberstam, J. (1998). *Female Masculinity*. Durham: Duke University Press.

Hefner, R. W. (1985). *Hindu Javanese: Tengger Tradition and Islam*. Princeton: Princeton University Press.

Hefner, R. W. (1987). The Politics of Popular Art: *Tayuban* Dance and Culture Change in East Java. *Indonesia*, 43, pp. 75–94.

Hegarty, B. (2017). The Value of Transgender: *Waria* Affective Labor for Transnational Media Markets in Indonesia. *TSG: Transgender Studies Quarterly*, 4(1), pp. 78–95.

Higginbotham, E. B. (1993). *Righteous Discontent: The Women's Movement in the Black Baptist Church, 1880–1920*. Cambridge, MA and London, UK: Harvard University Press.

Hughes-Freeland, F. (1993). *Golék Ménak* and *Tayuban*: Patronage and professionalism in two spheres of Central Javanese culture. In: B. Arps, ed., *Performance in Java and Bali: Studies of Narrative, Theatre, Music, and Dance*. London: School of Oriental and African Studies, University of London, pp. 88–120.

Hughes-Freeland, F. (1995). Performance and gender in Javanese palace tradition. In: W. J. Karim, ed., *"Male" and "Female" in Developing Southeast Asia*. Oxford: Berg Publishers, pp. 181–206.

Hughes-Freeland, F. (2006). Constructing a classical tradition: Javanese court dance in Indonesia. In: T. J. Buckland, ed., *Dancing from Past to Present: Nation, Culture, Identities*. Madison: The University of Wisconsin Press, pp. 52–74.

Hughes-Freeland, F. (2008a). Cross-Dressing across Cultures: Genre and Gender in the Dances of *Didik Nini Thowok*. Asia Research Institute Working Paper Series No. 108. Singapore: Asia Research Institute, National University of Singapore. Available at: www.ari.nus.edu.sg/publication_details.asp?pubtypeid=WP&pubid=1264 [accessed July 18, 2014].

Hughes-Freeland, F. (2008b). *Embodied Communities: Dance Traditions and Change in Java*. New York: Berghahn Books.

Hughes-Freeland, F. (2008c). Gender, Representation, Experience: The Case of Village Performers in Java. *Dance Research*, 26(2), pp. 140–167.

Isaka, M. (2016). *Onnagata: A Labyrinth of Gendering in Kabuki Theater*. Seattle and London: University of Washington Press.

Janarto, H. G. (2005). *Didik Nini Thowok: Menari Sampai Lahir Kembali.* [*Didik Nini Thowok: Dancing until Reborn.*] Malang: Sava Media; Yogyakarta: LPK Tari Natya Lakshita.

Jefferson, H. (2023). The Politics of Respectability and Black Americans' Punitive Attitudes. *American Political Science Review*, 117(4), pp. 1448–1464.

Kalanduyan, D. S. (1996). Magindanaon Kulintang Music: Instruments, Repertoire, Performance Contexts and Social Functions. *Asian Music*, 27(2), pp. 3–18.

Keeler, W. (1983). Shame and Stage Fright in Java. *Ethos*, 11(3), pp. 152–165.

Keeler, W. (1987). *Javanese Shadow Plays, Javanese Selves.* Princeton: Princeton University Press.

Keeler, W. (1990). Speaking of gender in Java. In: J. M. Atkinson and S. Errington, eds., *Power and Difference: Gender in Island Southeast Asia.* Stanford: Stanford University Press, pp. 127–152.

Lau, F. (2008). *Music in China: Experiencing Music, Expressing Culture.* New York and Oxford: Oxford University Press.

Li, S. L. (2003). *Cross-Dressing in Chinese Opera.* Hong Kong: Hong Kong University Press.

Manuel, P. (1988). *Popular Musics of the Non-Western World: An Introductory Survey.* New York: Oxford University Press.

Mendoza, Z. S. (2000). *Shaping Society through Dance: Mestizo Ritual Performance in the Peruvian Andes.* Chicago: University of Chicago Press.

Mrázek, J. (2005). Masks and Selves in Contemporary Java: The Dances of Didik Nini Thowok. *Journal of Southeast Asian Studies*, 36(2), pp. 249–279.

Mujiati. (2004). *Tari Beskalan Lanang: Karya Mohamad Soleh Adi Pramana Di Padepokan Seni Mangun Dharmo Desa Tulus Besar*

Kecamatan Tumpang Kabupaten Malang. [*Beskalan Lanang Dance: A Work of Mohamad Soleh Adi Pramana at the Mangun Dharmo Art Center in the Village of Tulus Besar, Subdistrict of Tumpang, Regency of Malang.*] Skripsi S-1. Surakarta: Sekolah Tinggi Seni Indonesia.

Mulder, N. (2005). *Mysticism in Java: Ideology in Indonesia.* Yogyakarta: Kanisius Publishing House.

Murtagh, B. (2011). *Gay, Lesbi* and *Waria* Audiences in Indonesia: Watching Homosexuality on Screen. *Indonesia and the Malay World,* 39(115), pp. 391–415.

Nash, J. C. (2008). Re-thinking Intersectionality. *Feminist Review,* 89, pp. 1–15.

Neuman, D. M. (1993). Epilogue: Paradigms and stories. In: S. Blum, P. V. Bohlman and D. M. Neuman, eds., *Ethnomusicology and Modern Music History.* Urbana: University of Illinois Press, pp. 268–277.

Oetomo, D. (1996). Gender and Sexual Orientation in Indonesia. In: L. J. Sears, ed., *Fantasizing the Feminine in Indonesia.* Durham: Duke University Press, pp. 259–269.

Oetomo, D. (2000). Masculinity in Indonesia: Genders, sexualities, and identities in a changing society. In: R. Parker, R. M. Barbosa and P. Aggleton, eds., *Framing the Sexual Subject: The Politics of Gender, Sexuality, and Power.* Berkeley: University of California Press, pp. 46–59.

Onghokham. (1972). The Wayang Topèng World of Malang. *Indonesia,* 14, pp. 110–124.

Pawestri, T. T. (2006). Transvesti *Pada Seni Pertunjukan Ludruk Malang.* [*Female Impersonators in Malang Ludruk Performances.*] Skripsi Sarjana Antropologi Tari. Institut Kesenian Jakarta.

Peacock, J. L. (1978). Symbolic reversal and social history: Transvestites and clowns of Java. In: B. A. Babcock, ed.,

The Reversible World: Symbolic Inversion in Art and Society. Ithaca: Cornell University Press, pp. 209–224.

Peacock, J. L. (1987). *Rites of Modernization: Symbolic and Social Aspects of Indonesian Proletarian Drama.* Chicago: The University of Chicago Press.

Peletz, M. G. (2006). Transgenderism and Gender Pluralism in Southeast Asia since Early Modern Times. *Current Anthropology*, 47(2), pp. 309–340.

Pigeaud, T. (1938). *Javaanse Volksvertoningen: Bijdrage tot de Beschrijving van Land en Volk.* Batavia: Volkslectuur.

Ponder, H. W. (1990). *Javanese Panorama: More Impressions of the 1930s.* Singapore: Oxford University Press.

Rabaka, R. (2012). Remix 2: "Lifting As We Climb!" Classic blues queens and the Black Women's Club movement, Neo-Soul Sistas and the Hip Hop Women's movement. In: *Hip Hop's Amnesia: From Blues and the Black Women's Club Movement to Rap and the Hip Hop Movement.* Lanham, Boulder, New York, Toronto, Plymouth, UK: Lexington Books, pp. 19–98.

Raffles, T. S. (1988). *The History of Java.* Vol. I. Singapore: Oxford University Press.

Rao, N. Y. (2002). Songs of the Exclusion Era: New York Chinatown's Opera Theaters in the 1920s. *American Music*, 20(4), pp. 399–444.

Robertson, J. (1998). *Takarazuka: Sexual Politics and Popular Culture in Modern Japan.* Berkeley, Los Angeles, and London: University of California Press.

Ross, L. M. (2005). Mask, Gender, and Performance in Indonesia: An Interview with Didik Nini Thowok. *Asian Theatre Journal*, 22(2), pp. 214–226.

Schrieber, K. E. (1991). *Power in the East Javanese Jaranan and Wayang Topeng.* MA thesis. University of Virginia, Charlottesville.

Sears, L. J. (2007). Postcolonial identities, feminist criticism, and Southeast Asian studies. In: L. J. Sears, ed., *Knowing Southeast Asian Subjects*. Seattle: University of Washington Press in association with Singapore: NUS Press, pp. 35–74.

Shaw, A. (2005). Changing Sex and Bending Gender: An Introduction. In: A. Shaw and S. Ardener, ed., *Changing Sex and Bending Gender*. New York: Berghahn Books, pp. 1–19.

Shiraishi, S. S. (1997). *Young Heroes: The Indonesian Family in Politics*. Ithaca: Southeast Asia Program, Cornell University.

Solander, T. (2023). Mortal Bromance: Homoeroticism on the Takarazuka Stage. *Asian Theatre Journal*, 40(1), pp. 96–120.

Spiller, H. (2007). Negotiating masculinity in an Indonesian pop song: Doel Sumbang's "Ronggeng". In: F. Jarman-Ivens, ed., *Oh Boy! Masculinities and Popular Music*. New York: Routledge, pp. 39–57.

Spiller, H. (2008). *Focus: Gamelan Music of Indonesia*. New York: Routledge.

Spiller, H. (2010). *Erotic Triangles: Sundanese Dance and Masculinity in West Java*. Chicago: The University of Chicago Press.

Stokes, M. (1994). Introduction: Ethnicity, identity and music. In: M. Stokes, ed., *Ethnicity, Identity and Music: The Musical Construction of Place*. Oxford: Berg Publishers, pp. 1–27.

Stoler, A. L., with Strassler, K. (2002). Memory-work in Java: A cautionary tale. In: A. L. Stoler, *Carnal Knowledge and Imperial Power: Race and the Intimate in Colonial Rule*. Berkeley: University of California Press, pp. 162–203.

Sumarsam. (1995). *Gamelan: Cultural Interaction and Musical Development in Central Java*. Chicago: The University of Chicago Press.

Sunardi, C. (2009). Pushing at the Boundaries of the Body: Cultural Politics and Cross-Gender Dance in East Java. *Bijdragen tot de Taal-, Land- en Volkenkunde*, 165(4), pp. 459–492.

Sunardi, C. (2010). Making Sense and Senses of Locale through Perceptions of Music and Dance in Malang, East Java. *Asian Music*, 41(1), pp. 89–126.

Sunardi, C. (2011). Negotiating Authority and Articulating Gender: Performer Interaction in Malang, East Java. *Ethnomusicology*, 55(1), pp. 31–54.

Sunardi, C. (2013). Complicating senses of masculinity, femininity, and Islam through the performing arts in Malang, East Java. In: T. P. Daniels, ed., *Performance, Popular Culture, and Piety in Muslim Southeast Asia*. New York: Palgrave Macmillan, pp. 135–160.

Sunardi, C. (2015). *Stunning Males and Powerful Females: Gender and Tradition in East Javanese Dance*. Urbana, Chicago and Springfield: University of Illinois Press.

Sunardi, C. (2017). Talking About Mode in Malang, East Java. *Asian Music*, 48(2), pp. 62–89.

Sunardi, C. (2020). A Mythical Medieval Hero in Modern East Java: The Masked Dance *Gunung Sari* as an Alternative Model of Masculinity. *Ethnomusicology*, 64(3), pp. 447–472.

Sunardi, C. (2022). Approaching the magnetic power of female-ness through cross-gender dance performance in Malang, East Java. In: A. McGraw and C. J. Miller, eds., *Sounding Out the State of Indonesian Music*. Cornell University Press Southeast Asia Program Publications, pp. 287–302.

Sunardi, C. (2023). The Pleasures of *Parikan* in Malang, East Java: An Analysis of Text and Music in the Dance *Ngremo Putri*. *Asian Music*, 54(2), pp. 6–37.

Sunardi, C. (in press). Speaking of the Spiritual: An Exploration of Knowledge and Pedagogy in Performing Arts in Malang, East Java. *Asian Theatre Journal*.

Supanggah, R. (2003). Campur Sari: A Reflection. *Asian Music*, 34(2), pp. 1–20.

Sutton, R. A. (1985). Musical Pluralism in Java: Three Local Traditions. *Ethnomusicology*, 29(1), pp. 56–85.

Sutton, R. A. (1991). *Traditions of Gamelan Music in Java: Musical Pluralism and Regional Identity*. Cambridge: Cambridge University Press.

Sutton, R. A. (1993). *Semang* and *Seblang*: Thoughts on music, dance, and the sacred in Central and East Java. In: B. Arps, ed., *Performance in Java and Bali: Studies of Narrative, Theatre, Music, and Dance*. London: School of Oriental and African Studies, University of London, pp. 121–143.

Sutton, R. A. (2002). *Calling Back the Spirit: Music, Dance, and Cultural Politics in Lowland South Sulawesi*. Oxford: Oxford University Press.

van Doorn-Harder, P. (2006). *Women Shaping Islam: Reading the Qur'an in Indonesia*. Urbana: University of Illinois Press.

Wade, B. C. (2005). *Music in Japan: Experiencing Music, Expressing Culture*. New York and Oxford: Oxford University Press.

Wahyudi, S. and Simatupang, G.R.L.L., eds. (2005). *Cross-Gender*. Idea of D. N. Thowok and Y. S. Supradah. Malang: Sava Media and Yogyakarta: LPK Tari Lakshita.

Weintraub, A. N. (2010). *Dangdut Stories: A Social and Musical History of Indonesia's Most Popular Music*. Oxford: Oxford University Press.

Weiss, S. (2003). *Kothong Nanging Kebak*, Empty Yet Full: Some Thoughts on Embodiment and Aesthetics in Javanese Performance. *Asian Music*, 34(2), pp. 21–49.

Weiss, S. (2006). *Listening to an Earlier Java: Aesthetics, Gender, and the Music of Wayang in Central Java*. Leiden: KITLV Press.

White, E. F. (2001). *Dark Continent of our Bodies: Black Feminism and the Politics of Respectability*. Philadelphia: Temple University Press.

Widodo, A. (1995). The Stages of the State: Arts of the People and Rites of Hegemonization. *RIMA*, 29(1 & 2), pp. 1–35.

Wieringa, S. (2002). *Sexual Politics in Indonesia*. New York: Palgrave Macmillan.

Williams, S. (2001). *The Sound of the Ancestral Ship: Highland Music of West Java*. Oxford: Oxford University Press.

Wolbers, P. (1989). Transvestism, Eroticism, and Religion: In Search of a Contextual Background for the Gandrung and Seblang Traditions of Banyuwangi, East Java. *Progress Reports in Ethnomusicology*, 2(6), pp. 1–21.

Wolbers, P. (1993). The *Seblang* and its music: Aspects of an East Javanese fertility rite. In: B. Arps, ed., *Performance in Java and Bali: Studies of Narrative, Theatre, Music, and Dance*. London: School of Oriental and African Studies, University of London, pp. 34–46.

Yampolsky, P. (1991). Indonesian popular music. Liner notes to *Music of Indonesia 2: Indonesian Popular Music: Kroncong, Dangdut, and Langgam Jawa*. Smithsonian/Folkways Recordings CD SF40056.

Zurbuchen, M. S. (2005). Historical memory in contemporary Indonesia. In: M. S. Zurbuchen, ed., *Beginning to Remember: The Past in the Indonesian Present*. Singapore: Singapore University Press in association with Seattle: University of Washington Press, pp. 3–32.

Discography

Aneka Gending Tari Malangan, Volume 2. [A Variety of Malangan Dance Compositions, Volume 2] (n.d.) Yogyakarta: Studio LPK Tari Natya Lakshita and Malang: Joyoboyo Studio. Audio cassette.

Videography

Tari Tradisional Malangan. (2003). Padepokan Seni Mangun Dharma. VCD.

Recommended further reading

Blackwood, E. (2010). *Falling Into the Lesbi World: Desire and Difference in Indonesia*. Honolulu: University of Hawai'i Press.

Boellstorff, T. (2005). *The Gay Archipelago: Sexuality and Nation in Indonesia*. Princeton: Princeton University Press.

Halberstam, J. (1998). *Female Masculinity*. Durham: Duke University Press.

Spiller, H. (2010). *Erotic Triangles: Sundanese Dance and Masculinity in West Java*. Chicago: The University of Chicago Press.

Sunardi, C. (2015). *Stunning Males and Powerful Females: Gender and Tradition in East Javanese Dance*. Urbana, Chicago and Springfield: University of Illinois Press.

Index

www.ingramcontent.com/pod-product-compliance
Lightning Source LLC
Chambersburg PA
CBHW071747270326
41928CB00013B/2829